Early Tejano Ranching

Early Tejano Ranching

Daily Life at Ranchos San José & El Fresnillo

ANDRÉS SÁENZ

Edited, with an introduction by Andrés Tijerina

Published by Texas A&M University Press, College Station
in association with
The University of Texas Institute of Texan Cultures at San Antonio

First Texas A&M University Press edition, 2001
Previous edition published by the University of Texas Institute of Texan Cultures
at San Antonio

Lesson plans, curriculum aids, and other educational resources to supplement this book
are available at *www.texancultures.utsa.edu/ranching*

The images herein and many other images of Texas subjects are in the Institute's photograph collection; call (210) 458-2298 for information about obtaining copies.

The paper used in this book meets the minimum requirements
of the American National Standard for Permanence
of Paper for Printed Library Materials, Z39.48-1984.
Binding materials have been chosen for durability.

Library of Congress Cataloging-in-Publication Data

Sáenz, Andrés, 1927–
    Early Tejano ranching in Duval County : the family
history of Ranchos San José and El Fresnillo / Andrés Sáenz;
edited, with introduction by Andrés Tijerina
    p. cm.
    Includes index (p.).
    ISBN 1-58544-134-1 (cloth); 1-58544-163-5 (pbk.)
    1. Mexican Americans—Texas—Duval County—History—
19th century. 2. Mexican Americans—Texas—Duval County.
5. Sáenz family. 6. Ranchers—Texas—Duval County —
History—19th century. 7. Ranchers—Texas—Duval County—
Biography. 8. Ranch life—Texas—duval CountyHistory—19th
century. 9. Duval County (Tex.)—Biography. 10. Duval County
(Tex.)—Social life and customs—19th century. I. Tijerina,
Andrés. II. Title.

F392.D9 s24 2001
976.4'4630046872073—dc21
                             2001033181

Contents

Rancho San Jose

Rancho El Fresnillo

Editor's Comments

by Andrés Tijerina

It has been my pleasure to serve as editor for this book about early Tejano pioneers. I am proud to be associated with the writings of my *tocayo* (namesake), Andrés Sáenz of Falfurrias, Texas, and I have truly enjoyed my

Dr. Andrés Tijerina

work. In my writing career, I have been asked many times for advice on publishing a book, and my advice is always the same, "First write it." Well, Don Andrés Sáenz wrote it, and his work was a unique collection of rare information. I can only imagine the obstacles this gentleman had to overcome to write his manuscript, but he completed it. He has written a book that many others have proposed, tempering his chronicle with objectivity, compassion, and a rare insight.

Andrés Sáenz is a scion of the two pioneering Texas families whom he describes, the López and the Sáenz. He was born on August 9, 1927, at the Rancho de Santa Cruz, in southern Duval County, Texas. His parents were Praxedis Sáenz and Ydolina

López, both raised on early Texas ranches. Andrés attended a ranch school on Rancho Vera Cruz, graduating from San Diego High School in 1945. He married Jovita Treviño of Alice, Texas, on February 3, 1953. During the Korean conflict, Mr. Sáenz served on the U.S.S. *Iowa* in Korea and in Europe. Upon his discharge from the Navy, he returned to South Texas and worked twenty years for the Falfurrias auto dealership. This was followed by another nineteen years as owner of Falfurrias Auto Supply, Inc. For personal avocations, Andrés taught Catholic Christian doctrine for twenty years and is a member of the Spanish-American Genealogical Association (S.A.G.A) in Corpus Christi, Texas.

In 1997 Andrés Sáenz responded to a public announcement about staff from the Institute of Texan Cultures (ITC) coming to San Diego in search of documents, photos, and stories of the pioneering Tejano families of South Texas. Having developed a keen sense of history while a member of the S.A.G.A., Don Andrés responded to the ITC announcement. He provided the Institute with an impressive set of manuscripts, the manuscripts that I have had the pleasure of editing. My goal has been to make the narrative readable while preserving the original content, compassion, and literary integrity of Mr. Sáenz.

Andrés Sáenz joins a small cadre of other writers who wrote Tejano ranch history before him. They include Fermina Guerra, author of "Mexican and Spanish Folklore and Incidents in Southwest Texas"; Jovita González, author of "Social Life in Cameron, Starr, and Zapata Counties"; Emilia Schunior Ramirez, author of *Ranch Life in Hidalgo County after 1850*; and Roberto M. Villarreal, who wrote "The Mexican-American Vaqueros of the Kenedy Ranch: A Social History." Most of these other writers produced their works as master's theses at various Texas universities under the tutelage of professors such as J. Frank Dobie. Andrés Sáenz did not have the advantage of a college education. Nonetheless, he wrote with the same meticulous care and research of the other authors. Most importantly, Mr. Sáenz and the other writers had a deep personal desire to preserve the history of their Tejano heritage—a heritage missing in the textbooks found in public schools. All wrote with the intention of passing on the knowledge to their families. And, amazingly, they wrote as if coordinated by some unseen hand to fit the pieces of a puzzle together for posterity. Indeed, each wrote basically the same story about his or her respective region of the South Texas Tejano ranching frontier. Guerra wrote about the *ranchos* in Laredo, Ramirez about the *ranchos* in Hidalgo County, González about the *ranchos* in the deep Rio Grande Valley, and Villarreal about the *vaqueros* in the Corpus Christi and Kenedy County area.

Sáenz's work fits into the geographic center of the others. His story is about the region in the counties of Jim Hogg, Brooks, and Duval. These counties were carved out of Nueces County in the 19th century. Together, these regional histories provide the modern reader with a story of the true Texas pioneers. Although written in different decades by writers unknown to each other, the various books present an amazingly cohesive story. With the present work, Andrés Sáenz takes his place among the authors of Tejano historiography.

Acknowledgments

by Andrés Sáenz

An acknowledgment of appreciation is made to all members of the López family, listed below, who willingly shared their knowledge. Their recall of events served in many instances not only to verify but also to elaborate on important details that were missing from other sources. Amazingly, details that were gathered from three sources completed some stories from beginning to end. I wish to thank the following:

Mr. Francisco López Jr. from Alice, Texas, for interviews from 1985 through 1991. He displayed a remarkable memory in relating events from his childhood, detailed conversations with his father, Francisco López Sr., about his grandfather José Antonio López, and extensive information on Texas history—including facts about the Spanish Colonial era in Texas.

Mr. Hector López, an attorney from Alice and the son of Francisco López Jr., for material from conversations with his father and also for his words of encouragement for me to continue with this history.

The **grandchildren of Fermán López: Mrs. Marina López López** from San Diego, Texas; and **Ricardo González López** from Corpus Christi, Texas.

Leopoldo López, a grandson of Pedro López from Alice, Texas.

Tomás Juan Benavides Jr., a great-grandson of Pedro López from Houston, Texas.

The **grandchildren of Jesús López** living at San Andrés.

Rodolfo López, a grandson of Margarito López from San José.

Teresa García Valadez from San José.

Hortencia Moya from Livingston, Texas.

Alejo López, a grandson of Francisco López, from San José.

Mrs. Lydia López Sáenz from Rancho El Mesquite Bonito.

And to the many other people whose conversations contributed information to this history, I express my appreciation.

I wish to give special recognition to F. Rene González from San Marcos, who married Amparo Valadez López, a granddaughter of Pedro López. Rene devoted many hours to editing and copying the manuscript. My thanks are also extended to my *Primo* for giving me the confidence to continue this history. I also wish to give special recognition to Mrs. Mira Smithwick, president of the Spanish American Genealogical Association (S.A.G.A.) of Corpus Christi, for offering inspiration and courage, putting the final manuscript on the computer, editing, and putting it into book format for presentation to the Institute of Texan Cultures. And, of course, I offer a very special thanks to my wife, Jovita, for helping with English words for some household items and for knowing the different materials used in the early years to make clothing. I am grateful to her for accompanying me on the many trips to cemeteries, to libraries, and to Mier, Camargo, and other places of interest to get the photographs. Finally, I owe a very special recognition to my mother, Ydolina, who not only was a gracious loving presence in our home during the last six and a half years of her life but who also shared the knowledge and experiences of her legendary life. Rest in peace, Mama. *Que en paz descanse, Mamá.*

Ydolina López Sáenz in 1981 next to a palm tree her parents planted when they built their first home on San José

Preface

by Andrés Sáenz

I wanted to know where my ancestors came from, why they came, how they came, how they obtained their land, how they made a living from the land, and finally how they went about passing it on to their heirs. I hope these

Andrés Sáenz

recollections will help others become aware of and appreciate the parcel of land that we have today through the sacrifices of our great-great-grandfathers and great-grandfathers, our *tatarabuelos* and *bisabuelos*. In this text, I have made an effort to obtain verifiable and documented information dating back to the 1860s.

The seed for this history grew from conversations with my mother, Ydolina López Sáenz, beginning in 1980 and continuing for six years. In evening porch conversations, she described how her family lived during her childhood and what she had learned from her father, Pedro, who had shared with her his life experiences and those of his father, An-

tonio, the original family settler. I wrote down many of these conversations as they occurred. When she passed away in 1987, I had sixty-five pages of manuscript that presented me with a challenge: my choice was either to write a book to share with the López family or to do nothing and let it be lost forever.

In appreciation of its value, I decided to pass on this history. I realized that a book required additional interviews to verify information. It also required genealogical information, which I obtained from microfilm at the Local History Department and through research facilitated by the S.A.G.A. at the Corpus Christi Public Library. I consulted the census reports for 1860, 1870, 1880, 1900, 1910, and 1920 available at the Corpus Christi Public Library. Tax assessment rolls for Nueces County starting with the year 1860 verified the first time the name Antonio López appeared with property. These tax assessment rolls listed abstract numbers with acreage for the land, the survey number, the number of acres, and a head count for horses, mules, cattle, sheep, goats, and other personal property. Additional information came from cemeteries at San José, La Bandera, Loma Alta, El Refugio, Las Latas, Calaveras, El Guajillo, and many others. I traveled to Ciudad Mier and Camargo in Mexico to research documents and church archives. I then compiled the information from my mother with pictures and documents. This account presents the legacy of my great-grandparents Antonio López and María de los Santos as a gift to all their descendants.

Introduction

by Andrés Tijerina

    South Texas was settled in the mid-1700s by Spanish and Mexican families who were brought to populate the region by the wealthy Spanish count José de Escandón. South Texas was under the Spanish flag as part of the frontier province of Nuevo Santander. Escandón founded his colony between the Pánuco River in present-day Mexico and the Guadalupe River in Texas. To provide for the settlement, he brought ranching families who, indeed, established the foundation of the American ranching industry.

    Escandón founded five municipalities along the Rio Grande: Laredo, Guerrero, Mier, Camargo, and Reynosa. To the Mexicans these were known jointly as Las Villas del Norte, the Villages of the North. The families who came north from the Rio Grande and settled the ranching frontier are the subjects of this book. Indeed, the Tejanos, that is, the original founders of Texas, were not immigrants as so many Americans see them. While many Texans today boast that Texas was once a republic, these ranching Tejano families are Texans who lived and served under all six of the Texas flags. Descendants of the early ranchers founded the Texas ranch towns of Dolores, Zapata, Cuevitas, San Diego, San Juan, Palito Blanco, Agua Dulce, El Sauz, Los Olmos, San Luis, Peñascal, San Ignacio, and Los Sáenz. In fact, all of these present-day towns were founded not as towns but as Tejano family ranches.

    Many modern Americans are confused about the origins of Tejanos because the borders of Texas moved, not the settlers. These early settlers now called Tejanos came before the area was part of Texas or the United States. Texas south of the Nueces River officially became part of the United States when the Treaty of Guadalupe Hidalgo ended the United States-Mexico War on February 8, 1848. The treaty established the Rio Grande as the southern boundary of Texas and the United States. By virtue of the treaty, Mexican citizens north of the Rio Grande became American citizens. Although the Mexican settlers became Texans and Americans by the treaty, they retained their strong cultural and family links to their original settlements of Las Villas del Norte located on the southern bank of the Rio Grande. At this time, the northern municipalities were incorporated into the State of Texas under United States jurisdiction, specifically as Nueces County.

The area of Nueces County that later became Duval County was originally populated by Mexican settlers who came north from the village of Mier on the Rio Grande. These settlers included ancestors of Mr. Sáenz who would establish Ranchos San José and El Fresnillo. Obtaining land grants from the municipality of Mier in the Mexican state of Tamaulipas, they crossed the Wild Horse Desert, known as Desierto Muerto, into present-day Duval County. These hardy settlers included Julian Flores, Encarnación García Pérez, Martiana Pérez de García, and other ranchers who established the Rancho San Diego on San Diego Creek (about 50 miles west of Corpus Christi) about 1815. Following them, Juan Bautista González and other settlers founded the ranches of La Rosita and El Palito Blanco and the Peñitas Ranch. Rancho San Diego eventually became a town with the same name. The neighboring ranch towns were Concepción, Realitos, and Piedras Pintas. In 1858 the Texas Legislature established the county of Duval, formally separating it from Nueces County in 1876.

Duval County lay at the crossroads of trade between San Antonio and Brownsville, Corpus Christi, and Laredo. Not surprisingly, the town of San Diego attracted stagecoach lines along those two routes. The trade routes were also used in moving stolen livestock, as well as contingents of the U.S. Army and Texas Rangers in pursuit of cattle rustlers. The ranches in this area became a production center for horses, cattle, and sheep. By the late 1850s, Duval County included the large cattle and sheep ranches of Las Conchas, La Trinidad, Santa Gertrudis, Petronilla, Mendieta, Veleño, and Lagarto. By 1880 the county was a major market, home to over a million sheep. Duval County ranches made Corpus Christi the nation's leading wool port. The county also became the point of origin of the famous cattle trails that took millions of Texas longhorn cattle north to Kansas and Missouri. About 1880 the Texas-Mexico Railway built a line from Corpus Christi, through San Diego, to Laredo, which expanded the role of Duval County as the crossroads of political and economic activity.

Duval County attracted unwanted visitors. Mexican rustlers raided area ranches in 1875. Hostile Indians staged a final raid on the county in 1878, killing several ranch workers. As a result of these raids, the State of Texas established a ranger station in San Diego. In 1888 Catarino Garza, a Mexican intellectual, recruited hundreds of local *rancheros* into an informal cavalry unit. Garza had married into the Pérez family of the Palito Blanco Ranch just north of the San José Ranch in Duval County. Opposed to the government of Mexican dictator Porfirio Díaz, Garza led his Ranchero Cavalry from Duval County into Mexico, where he conducted an extended military campaign against the Mexican army. He returned to the Palito Blanco Ranch, hotly pursued by the Texas Rangers, who found themselves unable to capture him. He eventually went to Cuba and other countries, where he continued to promote revolutions.

Meanwhile, the ranches of Duval County such as San José and El Fresnillo continued to develop economically. In the 1890s, railroads eclipsed cattle drives as a means of moving stock to market. The sheep industry shifted to West Texas. Compelled by necessity, the ranchers began the transition to commercial farming. Wool bales were replaced with cotton bales being transported to the cotton gins in San Diego and Corpus Christi. Cotton became the cash crop as Mexican settlers continued to migrate into Texas. Some came in search of work on the ranches, but others took advantage of the cheap land and the Texas land grant programs to establish themselves in the area.

The most dramatic political transition in Duval County occurred after the turn of the century. Anglo-American immigrants moved in, taking up land grants and buying the cheap ranch land. These newcomers used their political connections and their access to capital to take positions of power in the county governments and in the city of San Diego. This brought them into conflict with the Tejanos, the traditional Mexican–American leaders. In 1914 a political feud resulted in the shooting of three Mexican-American leaders in San Diego—an event that threatened to break out into outright warfare. The turmoil was averted by County Commissioner Archer Parr, an Anglo who sided with the Mexican Americans. By serving as intermediary, Parr effectively established a political machine that ruled the county for years. His local political control, however, was insufficient to prevent another regional movement. Hundreds of Mexican Americans issued the Plan de San Diego, a political declaration against the U.S. government calling for Mexican independence from Anglo power in South Texas. The U.S. Army dispersed the leader, Aniceto Pizaña, and his followers. The movement dissolved in 1916, but a strong political undercurrent of resistance continued among the area's Mexican-American citizenry.

Mexican-American citizens of Duval County continued to express dissatisfaction with their political status until the 1920s. By then the residents of the surrounding ranches and towns joined sociopolitical organizations that stood against Anglo power. In Duval County, the local newspaper, *The Bee (El Avispa)*, promoted civil and political rights for Mexican Americans. Many of the county's residents joined the League of Latin American Citizens, a Hispanic civil rights organization headquartered in Harlingen. Lawyer Alonso S. Perales led the group. They eventually merged with groups from San Antonio and Corpus Christi to form the League of United Latin American Citizens (LULAC). Founded in Corpus Christi in 1929, LULAC became a force in the Duval County area and grew to be the largest Hispanic civil rights organization in the United States. Thus, the ranch families that had come north to Duval County in the early 1800s provided leadership for the entire ranch country of South Texas. They developed the sheep and longhorn ranching industry of the nation, and they played a pivotal role not only in the revolution against the dictatorial government of Mexico but in the American civil rights movement as well.

As one reads the modest family stories of San José and El Fresnillo ranches, it is difficult to imagine that these were the same families who played so integral a role in the evolution of northern Mexico and southern Texas. Their imperatives appeared mundane, as they worked their ranches to survive the drought. But their struggles on the ranches should not blind the reader to the larger role that these pioneers played in the making of Texas. These humble pioneers, along with others, were the Texans who started the western cattle kingdom of more than five million longhorn cattle. They produced the longhorn herds that were driven on cattle trails to the northern railheads after the Civil War ended. Ironically, most Americans can name the cattle towns in Kansas and Missouri but know very little of the Tejano ranch families who founded the longhorn cattle industry which fed the nation. The following stories may sound like informal family legends, but they are deeply rooted in United States history. Without these ranch families, the history of the state of Texas would not be complete.

Genealogy Charts

Author Andrés Sáenz's
Ancestor Chart

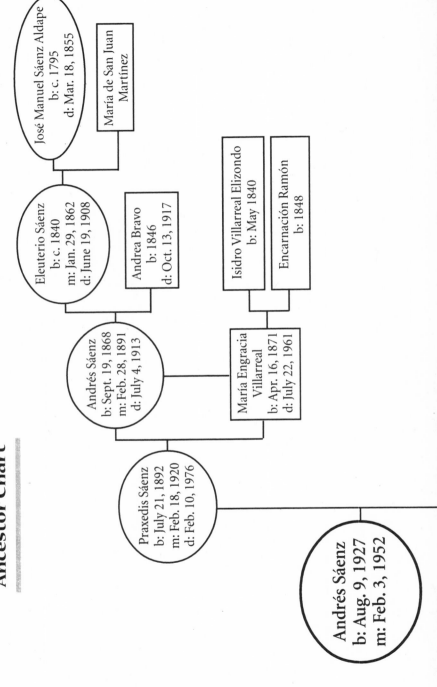

José Manuel Sáenz Aldape
b: c. 1795
d: Mar. 18, 1855

María de San Juan Martínez

Eleuterio Sáenz
b: c. 1840
m: Jan. 29, 1862
d: June 19, 1908

Andrea Bravo
b: 1846
d: Oct. 13, 1917

Isidro Villarreal Elizondo
b: May 1840

Encarnación Ramón
b: 1848

Andrés Sáenz
b: Sept. 19, 1868
m: Feb. 28, 1891
d: July 4, 1913

María Engracia Villarreal
b: Apr. 16, 1871
d: July 22, 1961

Praxedis Sáenz
b: July 21, 1892
m: Feb. 18, 1920
d: Feb. 10, 1976

Andrés Sáenz
b: Aug. 9, 1927
m: Feb. 3, 1952

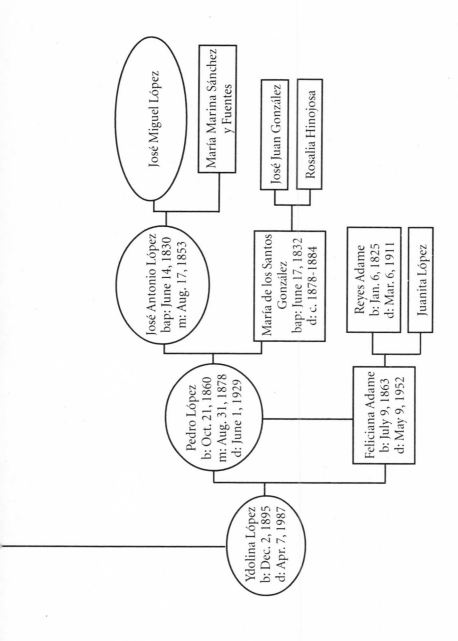

José Miguel López

María Marina Sánchez
y Fuentes

José Juan González

Rosalia Hinojosa

José Antonio López
bap: June 14, 1830
m: Aug. 17, 1853

María de los Santos
González
bap: June 17, 1832
d: c. 1878-1884

Reyes Adame
b: Jan. 6, 1825
d: Mar. 6, 1911

Juanita López

Pedro López
b: Oct. 21, 1860
m: Aug. 31, 1878
d: June 1, 1929

Feliciana Adame
b: July 9, 1863
d: May 9, 1952

Ydolina López
b: Dec. 2, 1895
d: Apr. 7, 1987

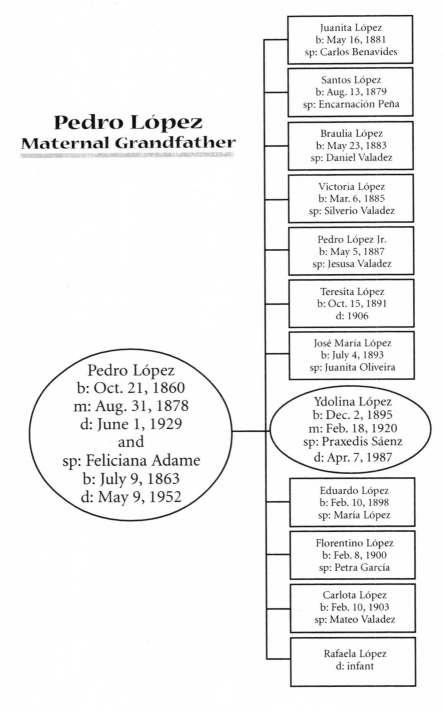

Pedro López
Maternal Grandfather

Pedro López
b: Oct. 21, 1860
m: Aug. 31, 1878
d: June 1, 1929
and
sp: Feliciana Adame
b: July 9, 1863
d: May 9, 1952

Juanita López
b: May 16, 1881
sp: Carlos Benavides

Santos López
b: Aug. 13, 1879
sp: Encarnación Peña

Braulia López
b: May 23, 1883
sp: Daniel Valadez

Victoria López
b: Mar. 6, 1885
sp: Silverio Valadez

Pedro López Jr.
b: May 5, 1887
sp: Jesusa Valadez

Teresita López
b: Oct. 15, 1891
d: 1906

José María López
b: July 4, 1893
sp: Juanita Oliveira

Ydolina López
b: Dec. 2, 1895
m: Feb. 18, 1920
sp: Praxedis Sáenz
d: Apr. 7, 1987

Eduardo López
b: Feb. 10, 1898
sp: María López

Florentino López
b: Feb. 8, 1900
sp: Petra García

Carlota López
b: Feb. 10, 1903
sp: Mateo Valadez

Rafaela López
d: infant

José Antonio López
Maternal
Great-Grandfather

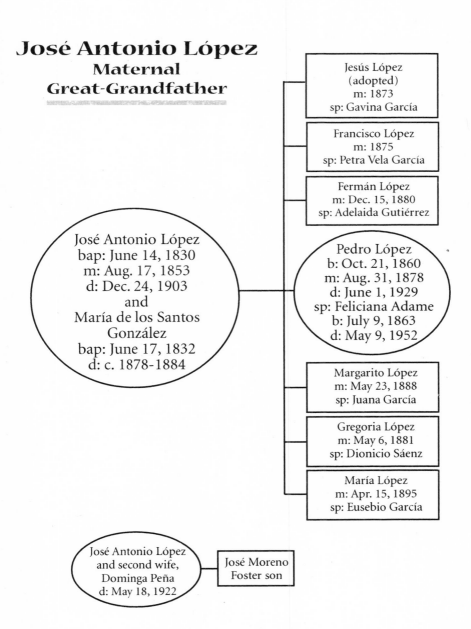

Jesús López
(adopted)
m: 1873
sp: Gavina García

Francisco López
m: 1875
sp: Petra Vela García

Fermán López
m: Dec. 15, 1880
sp: Adelaida Gutiérrez

José Antonio López
bap: June 14, 1830
m: Aug. 17, 1853
d: Dec. 24, 1903
and
María de los Santos
González
bap: June 17, 1832
d: c. 1878-1884

Pedro López
b: Oct. 21, 1860
m: Aug. 31, 1878
d: June 1, 1929
sp: Feliciana Adame
b: July 9, 1863
d: May 9, 1952

Margarito López
m: May 23, 1888
sp: Juana García

Gregoria López
m: May 6, 1881
sp: Dionicio Sáenz

María López
m: Apr. 15, 1895
sp: Eusebio García

José Antonio López
and second wife,
Dominga Peña
d: May 18, 1922

José Moreno
Foster son

José Miguel López
Maternal
Great-Great-Grandfather

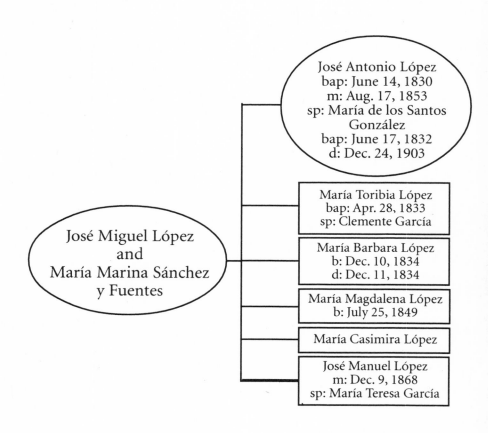

José Antonio López
bap: June 14, 1830
m: Aug. 17, 1853
sp: María de los Santos
González
bap: June 17, 1832
d: Dec. 24, 1903

María Toribia López
bap: Apr. 28, 1833
sp: Clemente García

María Barbara López
b: Dec. 10, 1834
d: Dec. 11, 1834

María Magdalena López
b: July 25, 1849

María Casimira López

José Manuel López
m: Dec. 9, 1868
sp: María Teresa García

José Miguel López
and
María Marina Sánchez
y Fuentes

Andrés Sáenz
Paternal Grandfather

Andrés Sáenz
b: Sept. 19, 1868
m: Feb. 28, 1891
d: July 4, 1913
and
María Engracia Villarreal
b: Apr. 16, 1871
d: July 20, 1961

Praxedis Sáenz
b: July 21, 1892
m: Feb. 18, 1920
sp: Ydolina López
d: Feb. 10, 1976

Eugenio Sáenz
b: Nov. 1893
m: Feb. 11, 1921
sp: Mariana González

Eleuterio Sáenz
b: Sept. 1895
m: July 4, 1929
sp: Zulema Palacios

Guadalupe Sáenz
b: Oct. 1897
m: 1936
sp: Hipólito Sáenz

Anastacia Sáenz
b: 1910
m: May 9, 1937
sp: Abelino Sáenz

Eustorgio Sáenz
m: Feb. 18, 1933
sp: Rosaura Sáenz

Florencia Sáenz

Natalia Sáenz
b: 1908
m: Aug. 27, 1927
sp: Daniel López

Andrés "Andrecito"
Sáenz Jr.
b: 1912
d: Mar. 14, 1914

Flavia Sáenz

Eleuterio Sáenz
Paternal
Great-Grandfather

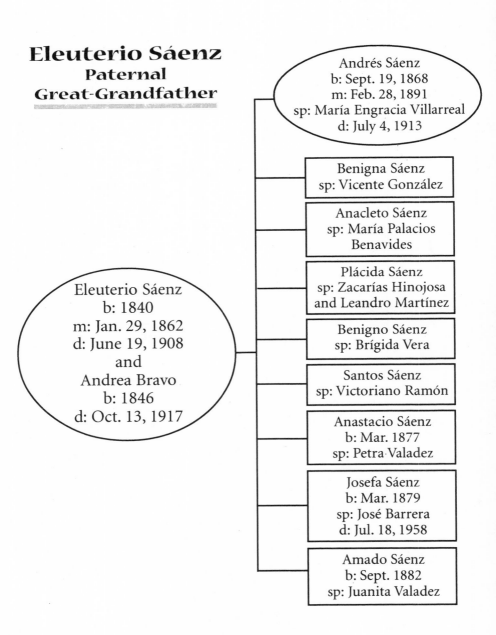

Andrés Sáenz
b: Sept. 19, 1868
m: Feb. 28, 1891
sp: María Engracia Villarreal
d: July 4, 1913

Benigna Sáenz
sp: Vicente González

Anacleto Sáenz
sp: María Palacios
Benavides

Plácida Sáenz
sp: Zacarías Hinojosa
and Leandro Martínez

Benigno Sáenz
sp: Brígida Vera

Santos Sáenz
sp: Victoriano Ramón

Anastacio Sáenz
b: Mar. 1877
sp: Petra·Valadez

Josefa Sáenz
b: Mar. 1879
sp: José Barrera
d: Jul. 18, 1958

Amado Sáenz
b: Sept. 1882
sp: Juanita Valadez

Eleuterio Sáenz
b: 1840
m: Jan. 29, 1862
d: June 19, 1908
and
Andrea Bravo
b: 1846
d: Oct. 13, 1917

Maps

LAS VILLAS DEL NORTE

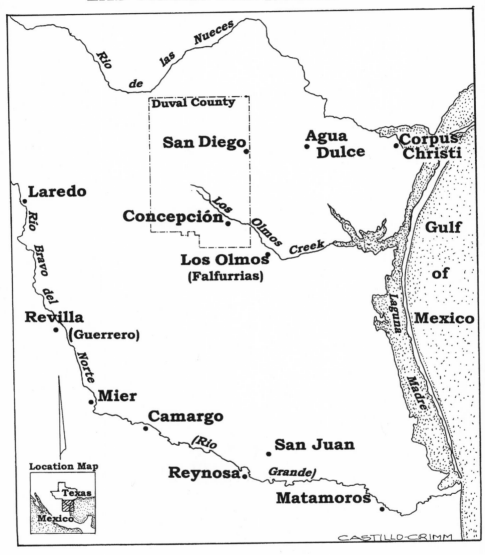

RANCHOS SAN JOSÉ,
EL FRESNILLO, AND VICINITY

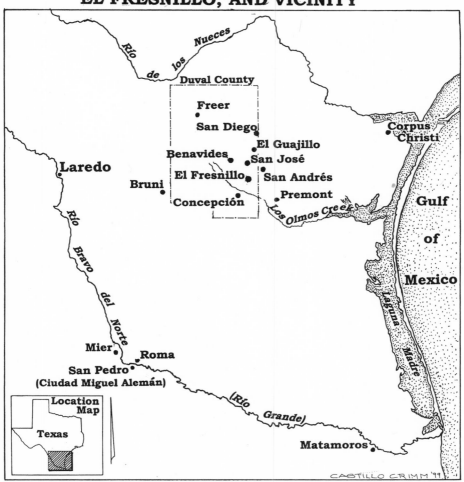

RANCHO
SAN JOSÉ

Dominga Peña and José Antonio López, c. 1890

*(No photograph is available of
Antonio's first wife, María de los Santos González,
who died sometime between 1878 and 1884.)*

1

Travels North

The founders of Rancho San José were José Antonio López and his wife, María de los Santos González.[1] Antonio and María were married in

José Antonio López

Mier on August 17, 1853, at the Church of the Immaculate Conception (La Parroquia de la Inmaculada Concepción). Antonio's parents were José Miguel López and María Marina Sánchez y Fuentes. María de los Santos's parents were José Juan González and Rosalía Hinojosa. During the 1860s, Antonio and María lived in San Pedro, which is now Ciudad Miguel Alemán in the state of Tamaulipas, Mexico. Their home is described as a stone house, a *casa de piedra*, or a house constructed of *sillares*, large blocks of limestone or sandstone from the surrounding region.

The people who lived in this type of house at the time were rich landowners, *hacendados*, ranchers who owned a considerable amount of land and raised cattle, sheep, goats, and horses.[2] Old photographs of San Pedro taken across the bridge from Roma, Texas, show a few of the *sillar* houses and many *jacales*, thatched-roof huts constructed of tree logs in which the majority of the people lived.

---

[1] Rancho San José was a family farm where many members of the family eventually had homes. It never became a village or incorporated community.

[2] The word *hacendado* refers to Mexican ranchers who had received large land grants on which they maintained big stock-raising operations. It has strong social connotations of power and grandeur, as these men ruled over the families as well as the economics of their large estates.

3

The main purpose of this history is to pursue certain questions I had about my family background. When did the family move to Texas and establish the Rancho San José? Where did Antonio get his wealth? Was it an inheritance from his father? Documents in the History Archives of Mier, Archivo Histórico de Mier, in Tamaulipas, Mexico, answered some of these questions.[3]

About the 1860s, when the López family lived in Mexico, Chico Reyna, a cousin of Antonio's, made trips hauling wool from Cadereyta, Nuevo León, through General Bravo, Nuevo León, and on to Corpus Christi, Texas. On his way through, he stopped to rest and visit with Antonio in San Pedro. Chico hauled his wool in a cart train, or *tren de carretas*, consisting of three two-wheeled carts. A strong lead rope made of rawhide held the carts together as they traveled. Oxen pulled the carts, which had bowed wooden arches covered with canvas. The oxen were fed, watered, and rested for the night at Antonio's ranch so they would be ready to go the next morning.

On one of these trips, Francisco López, Antonio's oldest son, joined his uncle for the trip, little realizing the adventure that awaited him. The experience proved unforgettable for Francisco because there were so many new places to see. He later described the trip to his son, Francisco Jr. He found the speed of travel very slow and boring but steady. The oxen would keep on going and going. Francisco would walk for a while and then ride on the carts for a while. Occasionally, Chico prodded the oxen with a fancy decorated stick, a *garrocha*. The cart trails were sandy in places and rocky in others, making for a rough ride. Francisco observed that his uncle knew where to stop to

Old sillar *house near El Sauz*

[3] The house where Antonio and his family lived was later shown to Francisco López Jr. by his father in the early 1920s. By 1920 the house was within the town of San Pedro.

rest, to eat, and to water the oxen at the lagoons and creeks alongside the trail. Along the way they passed through some isolated ranches. Most consisted of *sillar* houses with one or two *jacales* nearby. His uncle knew most of the people living at the ranches, and he stopped briefly to talk to them. All of the ranches had names and served as landmarks in the area.

Jacal de leña

Years later Francisco drove along the road in a vehicle and remembered the *sillar* homes. When new roads bypassed the old homes, their names as landmarks were no longer known. Some of the houses can still be seen in ruins alongside the road from El Sauz to Rancho Randado. A few of the old ranches had two or three of the *sillar* homes.

On the small ranches, the stock consisted mainly of sheep and goats, a few cattle, and one or two horses to pull the buggy and provide transportation. Francisco remembered that the largest ranch was Rancho Randado, which had several of the *sillar* houses and many *jacales*. The *jacales* housed the working ranch hands known as *peones*.

Francisco saw earthen dams called *presas*. The ranchers made the *presas* by blocking the water flow of a creek with a ridge of dirt, un *bordo de tierra*. In some of the *presas*, an excavation was dug into the side wall and the dirt was used to build a ledge, giving it more depth so it would hold more water and form a small lake to provide water for a longer time for the livestock. These large ranches had cattle pens of mesquite logs, *corrales de leña*. A few ranches today have preserved this type of corral.

Another ranch that Francisco remembered very well was San Lorenzo. Later, though it's not known why, the name of this ranch was changed to Las Latas. His uncle usually made a late sleep stop there. Francisco came to know the owners, Albino and Crisanto Vela, well. They were very friendly, and he developed a good relationship with them. At that time, it was a very busy ranch, a landmark in the community. It included some *sillar* houses and many *jacales*. From the 1860s to about the 1920s, this ranch was a thriving community. There is nothing left of Las Latas today except a nearby cemetery with the names of the early pioneer families engraved on the tombstones. Other ranch families in the surrounding area had ancestors who started working at Las Latas when they came from Mexico and later went on to claim their own surveys of land.

Don Faustino "Chato" Vela owned a ranch close to Antonio's (in Mexico) and was the father of José María, Crisanto, Albino, and Teresa. Antonio talked with Chato and was aware that the Velas at Rancho Las Latas did well with their sheep and goat herds, *ganado menor*. In the early 1860s, they had just started adding cattle to their ranch stock. According to the tax assessment rolls of Nueces County for those years, the Vela family owned thousands of acres of land and had about 2,500 head of sheep, as well as goats, cattle, and horses. They had many shepherds working for them and other people clearing the land to raise crops.[4]

Francisco's first trip to Corpus Christi was a memorable experience for him. When he returned home, he was anxious to tell his father all about his trip and all he saw at Rancho Randado, at the busy Vela ranch, and the large herds of sheep, goats, cattle, and horses. The seaport he saw was a busy place for exporting wool, animal hides, and tallow. The stench of the hides and the tallow was terrible.

Francisco was eager to go on the next trip to Corpus Christi. The next time, he took extra clothes because he wanted to stay at the Vela Ranch until his uncle returned from Corpus Christ.

---

[4] Information on the Vela family provided by Francisco López Jr.

2

Moving North

Soon Antonio began thinking of expanding to this new land. He prepared himself for the trip and started following the cart trails towards Rancho Las Latas. On the way, he studied the terrain and the different types of ranches that he passed. He visited for a few days at Las Latas with the Vela family and made trips around the area looking for good land for pasture, *tierra de agostadero*, where he could establish a ranch. He checked into the possibility of buying land and moving his family to increase his landholdings and stock. For each family member, additional land could be obtained. He noticed also the abundance of wild horses. He later told his family that those wild horses were the major reason he decided to move to this new land.

In 1866 Antonio brought his wife and family to Rancho Las Latas. They stayed in the *jacales* of the Vela family. Some of the older members of his family started working with the Velas while he traveled back and forth to his ranch in San Pedro. He still had to tend to the San Pedro *rancho* in Mexico while trying to acquire land to establish his new ranch. Antonio López first appears on the Nueces County tax assessment rolls in 1869 as owning only sheep. He worked on the grazing land he had leased. By 1872, although he owned no land on record, he owned 35 horses. In 1873 he had 65 horses valued at $735 and four cows valued at $40.

Members of his family knew Antonio loved horses because he consistently owned more horses than other livestock. He taught his sons to ride bucking broncs at an early age by mounting his young sons on the bare backs of semitrained horses. All they had to hold on to was the horse's mane. When there were no more wild horses to capture, he raised his own horses to break, train, and sell. Family stories and his public affidavit indicate that he sold tamed saddle horses throughout his working life.

In order to capture wild horses that were running loose in the open pastures, a trap, or *trampa*, was used. The *trampa* consisted of two fences made of mesquite logs that angled toward the entrance to both a corral and a fenced area around the corral. A post supporting large mesquite branches served as a barrier along the longer of the two fences. The second stretch of fence was about half the length of the first. A group of wild horses was led slowly along the longer of the two fences until they were between the two fences. The cowboys then closed in until all the horses were inside the corral. Large logs were used to close the entrance.

The corral led to other fenced enclosures used to separate the horses the cowboys wanted to keep from the horses they let go. A shallow lagoon north of Antonio's house and several round, manmade waterholes, *tinajas*, provided water for the animals. When the water in the lagoon got low, the *tinajas* held water at the enclosures. Farther to the north was a pasture for the horses to feed on.

The men observed small groups of horses at the waterholes to see if they could pick one or two that met the overall natural beauty they were seeking in a horse. They maneuvered to isolate the horses with fine stature, good muscle, shiny coats, or a beautiful mane and tail from the rest of the group.

Once out in the open, the cowboys worked in pairs as a team. Two of them chased the horse in a circular direction. Then two more continued the chase to get the horse tired. The final two cowboys each roped the horse and pulled it in two different directions in order to stop it and control it.

These horses were worked, broken, and mounted in a round corral made of mesquite logs, *corral de leña redondo*. These round corrals were made strong and solid enough to keep the horses contained and to hold the cowboys standing or sitting on the fence. One of the corrals built at Rancho El Bordo was still standing in the 1980s.

Antonio loved horses, and he must have either been a good horse trainer or hired professional people to break these horses for him. The daily task of breaking horses required dedicated people who loved the dangerous work and had the patience to deal with the savage, brute animals. It took understanding and compassion to learn from each experience and improve their techniques because each animal behaved differently. The horses were always fed and cared for before the cowboys themselves ate.

After breaking and taming the horses, the cowboys took them in herds, *manadas*, to sell as saddle horses. A *manada* of horses or mares usually consisted of eleven animals.

In 1877 Antonio owned two tracts of land totaling 1,200 acres valued at $640 and sixteen horses valued at $160, along with a wagon, cattle, sheep, goats, and other personal property. By 1880 his listings were as follows: Abstract #586: 640 acres; Abstract #587: 640 acres from Seal & Morris, one wagon at $30, fifty horses at $300, fifteen cows at $120, 500 sheep at $500, 100 goats at $100, and other personal property at $20. Antonio may have sold his property at San Pedro but kept his house for visits to family. He continued to add to his landholdings, surveying and recording his homestead claims. In 1884 he obtained another section of land and another 320 acres adjacent to his landholdings on San José.[5] On a public affidavit dated December 10, 1886, Antonio listed the following property: 640 acres of land, forty mares, twenty fillies, seven saddle horses, seven colts, forty-eight cows, and eight yearlings.

---

[5] Information from conversations of Francisco López Jr. with his father, Francisco Sr.

3
Homesteading on Rancho San José

When Antonio López came to San José, there were two houses made of *sillares* on Rancho San Andrés. Architectural studies for the area indicate this type of house was constructed during the 1820s.[6] In this case, the houses were constructed before land grants were issued. Who built or lived in these houses is not known. When Antonio bought the land, he may have lived in one, because he dug a well about 300 feet south, close to a wash, a *derramadero*, where water flowed from a higher elevation to lower land. He struck water at a depth of thirty-five feet, but it was salty. So the family used the water only for washing clothes. Today this old well is covered with heavy boards and sheets of tin with dirt on top. It is still visible from a road nearby. A reliable water source was important in deciding a homesite. As soon as Antonio moved to his homestead, he began to provide it with life-giving water.

After digging the first well, Antonio hired people to dig another well located about three-quarters of a mile southwest of the first. He chose the area because it was close to a lagoon, probably reasoning that the water table would be shallower there. The second well lies about a half mile south/southwest of present-day San José. Workers built the upper structure of white limestone cemented with sand and lime. In the 1940s, concrete was added around the upper part of the structure. This supported the heavy, thick boards placed over the top to keep anyone from falling into the well. The water in this well was good for drinking, so Antonio built his house about twenty-five yards south of the well. It was

---

[6] Eugene George, *The Historic Architecture of Texas: the Falcón Reservoir* (Austin: Texas Historical Commission, 1975).

a medium-sized dwelling built with a porch to the west. His son Margarito also built his house close to the well in a westerly direction. Part of Margarito's house stands today. Rodolfo, a grandson of Margarito, said that, after a good rain, the lagoon filled and water in the well would rise almost to the top.

The family completed a third well, also dug by hand, about a half mile from the same underground stream, the *derramadero*, though a bit closer to the lagoon. This third well was over fifty feet deep and also produced good drinking water. Today it provides water for the Catholic Church on San José. The well has been modernized by cementing the upper structure and adding an electric pump. Pedro hand-dug this well with the help of his family—Pedro Jr., Eduardo, José María, and Florentino—and other people who were working for Pedro at the time.

While digging the third well, Eduardo was at the bottom and wanted to bring out a load of rock. The mule pulling the load fell and was dragged by the weight almost into the opening of the well. The results, of course, would have been disastrous if the mule had fallen into the well on top of Eduardo.[7]

This well, like the others, had two mesquite posts with a crossbeam holding a pulley, or *carrillo*. A rope held a large water bucket, or *cubo*. Men on horseback pulled the *cubo* from the well. The well provided water for the livestock as well as for home use. At Pedro's house, it took two people to draw water from the well: one person on horseback pulled the bucket out of the water, and another emptied the water into the troughs for watering the sheep, goats, and cattle. The men also filled barrels of water for drinking and, when necessary, for watering the rows of onions; garlic; tomatoes; green peppers; pumpkins; squash, or *calabazas*; cucumbers; and sweet potatoes that grew in the garden.

The family stored water for home consumption in wooden barrels, *barricas*. Water troughs, *canoas*, were made of heavy wooden planks. About 1910 Pedro installed a cylinder pump in the well and placed a heavy forked log by its side. This long mesquite log served as a lever to lift the rod from the pipes that ran to the water level of the well. About two years later, a windmill was set over the well to pump the water. This windmill worked well until 1919, when a storm destroyed it. At night the sheep

---

[7] Information is from Pedro López to his grandson Tomás Juan Benavides Jr.

and goats in corrals were given water from the well, but the demand for water for the livestock was not excessive. In those years, many of the lagoons held water almost year-round. Some creeks that ran through the pasture also had water flowing year-round.

The López's made regular trips to visit relatives in San Pedro, across the Rio Grande from Roma, Texas. The family sent messages of deaths, funerals, and mar-

From left, *Flavia, Anastacia, Natalia, and Guadalupe, daughters of Andrés and María Engracia Villarreal Sáenz leaning on the mesquite log lever used to pump water on El Fresnillo, c. 1925*

riages back and forth in a method developed by other settlers who had relatives in Guardado de Arriba and Guardado de Abajo. Someone would shout that so-and-so was very sick or had died to another person across the river, who relayed the message to a relative.

A trip by horseback from the ranch to San Pedro took about four days each way. Pedro made several trips to visit relatives. On the way back, he would stop to visit his close friend, Octaviano Escobar, at Rancho Las Ojas near Escobares. Octaviano had a *casa de sillares* and several *jacales* around his home. A rock house, a *casa de piedra*, still stands on this land.[8]

---

[8] The current descendants of Mr. Escobar know much about the people who lived in Rancho La Bandera and San José.

4

Sheepshearing

The busiest time for sheep ranchers was the sheepshearing season, *la temporada de la trasquila*. Sheepshearing season each year was around the month of April. The ranchers sought the advice of older, more experienced ranchers who determined from signs of nature that the winter season was over. Their main purpose was to avoid a freeze after the sheep were sheared. When this happened, unfortunate ranchers could easily lose their entire flock. The dead carcasses then had to be burned because the ranchers could not dig holes big enough to bury them. A man who rented a ranch near Palo Blanco between Falfurrias and Hebronville lost his flock in such a freeze. The owner of the land had a difficult time getting the owner of the sheep to clean up the mess.[9]

The sheep were kept in a natural corral, a *majada*. Ponciano, Pedro's brother-in-law, lived for a while in a *majada* about a half mile west of San José. The *majada* stood on the high ground of the pasture belonging to Pedro, Antonio's son. It was close to a fourth water well the family had dug. The sheep stayed in pens during the night at this spot. A heavy concentration of cactus and brush obstructed the place. It may be that the prickly cactus leaves were thrown around the fence to grow thick and serve as a fence also. A single clearing provided an entrance to the *majada*. All the mesquite trunks and logs from this corral have deteriorated, leaving only the heavy growth of cacti and trees. Indeed, only a lone mesquite tree in the center of this clearing remains, and it never grew to full size. No grass would grow in the area that once served as a corral. It is possible

---

[9] Information provided by Francisco López Jr. from conversations with his father, Francisco Sr.

that the sheep and goat excrement ruined the soil to a degree that it will not produce vegetation even to this day.

Ponciano slept under a lean-to that faced south. To construct the lean-to, men stacked a few logs over each other at the low end, placed two vertical posts on the south end, and laid a log horizontally across the top. The roof was made of mesquite branches. The entanglement of mesquite branches was heavy and solid. It could withstand the cold winter nights and serve as shelter from the sun and rain. Log walls stood at both ends. The floor was cleared on the north end to make room for sleeping. The lean-to was set up close to the only gate into the corral, allowing the shepherd to keep a close eye on the flock. Ponciano had some good dogs to help watch for predators at night. He did some light cooking, hanging his cooking utensils on the nearby tree branches between meals. Family members visited daily from San José, bringing him meals to reheat. Ponciano later moved to Kingsville, where he lived and raised his family.

Shearing sheep was a major operation in those days. The sheepshearers worked in a squatting position, which was painful to their legs and knees and cut off the circulation. They remained alert to the sheep's movements so as not to cut or stab it with the sharp points of the shearing scissors, *tijeras tacincas*. Another painful part for the shearer was the repetitive squeezing of the scissor blades, which were spring-loaded. Tension on the cutting edges made them very hard to close. The shearers got sore hands, sore arms, and very painful wrists. They wrapped leather straps around their wrists to ease the pain—they said that their wrists felt like they were split open. The first few days, the shearing went slowly. After a week or two, however, strong, experienced shearers could shear 100 sheep a day, earning $3.00 a day. They were paid 3 cents a head at the time. The earnings provided incentive for ranchers to enter the sheep and wool industry in South Texas.

Sheepshearing crew

5

The Children of José Antonio López and María de los Santos

José Antonio López and his wife, María de los Santos González, raised seven children: Jesús, Francisco, Fermán, Pedro, Margarito, Gregoria, and María.

Jesús López, the oldest, was adopted when the family lived at Las Latas. Jesús claimed his last name was García. Some people knew who his parents were, but his name was never officially recorded. He lived at Las Latas until after the 1890s, when he and his family moved to Rancho San Andrés near San José. He lived in a *sillar* home, the only *sillar* home still standing in the area today.

Francisco López, the oldest natural son of Antonio and María de los Santos, also lived at Las Latas. Later he lived briefly on Rancho San José.[10] After a drought in the late 1890s, he moved to a tract of land that he owned between Freer and Bruni. There he established a ranch that he named El Bordo, because it was on a high ridge of land dividing two bodies of water, Los Olmos Creek and the Río de las Nueces. He managed to buy more than 3,000 acres in the area.[11]

Fermán López lived east of Rancho El Guajillo. The area of land close to his ranch is called El Refugio. Directly to the east stand the remains of the two-story house of his father-in-law, Rafael Gutiérrez. Fermán built a ten-room ranch house.[12] Years later he moved his home to Rancho Loma Alta, where he lived with his family in his later years.

---

[10] San José was the López farm or ranch where many members of the family had homes.

[11] Information is from Francisco López Jr. to his grandson Alejo López.

[12] Marina López López of San Diego owns a photograph of this house.

Pedro López, my grandfather, lived on San José all his life. He built his home there, raised his family, and increased his landholdings through many years of hard work. Pedro built his house of lumber near the third well close to the church on San José today.

Margarito López lived on San José across the road from his father, Antonio's, house. He and his family worked hard to improve his land. His sons helped clear the land for planting.

Gregoria López also lived on Rancho San José. Her house stood just across the road and to the south of Pedro's house. She and her husband, Dionicio Sáenz, cleared some land for a field, built a home, and raised their family there.

María López lived a short distance to the north of San José on the land she inherited. She and her husband, Eusebio García, raised beef cattle. Their daughter, Josefina, married Juan Sandoval.

José Moreno was a foster son raised by Antonio during his second marriage to Dominga Peña. José lived near Antonio's house but later moved to Oilton, Texas.

In the early 1880s, the brothers Jesús, Francisco, Pedro, and Fermán, who were in their twenties, started to acquire their own stock. Like their father, they had a love for horses. They learned to tame horses and became hard-riding cowboys. By 1879 Pedro, Jesús, and Francisco had their own horses, sheep, goats, and other personal property. Fermán was the most enterprising of Antonio's children. He eventually owned a great deal of land, livestock, and even property lots in the city of San Diego, Texas.[13]

Antonio's first wife, María de los Santos, died sometime between 1878 and 1884 at the home of their adopted son, Jesús, who lived at Rancho Las Latas. She died of a carbuncle-type sore called a *grano carbunco* or *carbunclo*. This type of sore had a black center core that got hard. It was a painful malignant tumor, and the area around the sore turned reddish from the infection. The sore was located on the back of her neck and created complications. A present-day medical doctor consulted about this type of sore said that if the patient was a diabetic or was in poor health, the sore could cause death. It is believed that María de los Santos was

---

[13] Tax Assessment Rolls: Nueces County.

buried in the cemetery at Las Latas.[14] Pedro's mother-in-law, Juanita López Adame, died of this same type of sore.

By the time of Antonio's second marriage to Dominga Peña in 1886, most of his children had married:

- ◆ Jesús married Gavina García in 1873.
- ◆ Francisco married Petra Vela in 1875.
- ◆ Pedro married Feliciana Adame on August 31, 1878.
- ◆ Fermán married Adelaida Gutiérrez on December 15, 1880.
- ◆ Gregoria married Dionicio Sáenz on May 6, 1881.
- ◆ Margarito married Juana García on May 23, 1888.
- ◆ María married Eusebio García on April 15, 1895.

The 1900 census listed Antonio as age sixty-eight and his wife, Dominga, as age fifty-three, living in Duval County. At the time, they

were living on San José with Cleofas López and his wife, Victoriana.

Antonio López had a brother named José Manuel López, who married María Teresa García on December 9, 1868. Their sister María Magdalena visited Antonio in 1880. She is described as having a ruddy complexion. Another sister was María Casimira López. Indeed, Antonio may have had other brothers and sisters, but there was a discrepancy over the last name of María Marina, who was listed as Hinojosa. This could have been an error of the priest, which was very common.[15]

José Antonio Lopez with his second wife, Dominga Peña, 1890

---

[14] Antonio's granddaughter Ydolina states that María de los Santos González López was buried at the Las Latas cemetery, but the gravesite is unknown. However, there are two side-by-side tombs encircled in iron that are close to the tomb of Gavina García, Jesús' wife. It is probable that these two unmarked tombs belong to María de los Santos González López and Juanita López Adame.

[15] U.S. Bureau of the Census Manuscripts for Texas: 1880, 1890.

6

Antonio's Last Days at San José

Antonio was of slender build and had a ruddy complexion, blue-gray eyes, and red hair. At seventy-nine he suffered from angina and could not engage in heavy work but kept himself busy at a slow pace doing small detail work at the ranch. He rarely wore a coat on cold winter mornings because he said his body could stand cold weather. In his last years, he would walk the quarter mile from his house on Rancho San José early in the morning to wake up the family. He would tell them to get up because it was not cold. Since he had no set hours to work, he often visited his sons and daughters: Margarito, Gregoria, Pedro, María, and Jesús at Rancho San Andrés.

Antonio used to recite poems. Only a few were written. His family found a poem among his personal belongings after his death. It is almost a farewell or an epitaph—

Aquí yace una existencia,	Here lies an existence
El que siete décadas tuvo,	That lasted seven decades.
Que la que a su lado estuvo,	May the one who he had by his side,
Adolorida por su ausencia,	Grieved by his absence,
Recoja el polvo y la esencia,	Pick up the dust and the essence
Que su espíritu contuvo.	That his spirit contained.

Antonio died the morning of December 24, 1903, of heart complications. In 1895, prior to his marriage to his second wife, Dominga Peña, he had divided his land. At the time of his death, the homestead consisted of 200 acres plus an additional 30 acres. In 1904 his will provided 28.75 acres for each of his seven children and 28.75 for his wife, Dominga. Of each 28.75-acre parcel, a quarter acre was to provide for a gravesite; thus, two acres were set apart for a cemetery on the southwest corner of his property that is called the Antonio López Cemetery. His body rests there. Beside his gravestone stands a wooden grotto, which had been attached to an early wooden marker. The grotto contains the poem behind a hinged glass door. His great-grandson Reynaldo, who has now passed away, kept a freshly written copy of the poem in the grotto. Now Reynaldo's brother, Rodolfo, replaces the poem at the cemetery.[16] Dominga died on May 18, 1922. She too is buried at the Antonio López Cemetery.

---

[16] Reynaldo López's brother, Rodolfo, provided the copy of the poem.

7

The Droughts of 1894 and 1897

A drought occurred about 1894. All the members of the López family who had livestock suffered greatly and came very close to losing all they had worked so hard to obtain. They gathered their stock and drove them towards the open land west of Freer, near Bruni. At the end of the first day's ride, they camped for the night. At midnight it started to rain. All were soaked. The next morning, they continued their drive west towards Freer. Rain continued to fall all day. They camped that night in the rain, and the next morning they turned around and started home.[17]

Another drought occurred about 1897. Again the López brothers, Francisco, Pedro, Jesús, and Margarito, gathered the stock and headed out for different pastures in the same direction as in 1894. The land was open range owned by the state. When they began pasturing their livestock, some of the people in the area started staking out the land claims in the public domain. Through a state program, parcels of land were being sold. Francisco acquired enough parcels to provide for their livestock. He staked his land on a ridge that separated the high rocky terrain from the lower land to the north and called his ranch El Bordo.

The first thing they did on the new land was to establish a camp. They built a shaded area, or *portal*, to provide protection from the hot sun. Then they enclosed the sides to build a *jacal*, using the wood in the area. Here they slept and cooked meals for the cowhands and shepherds who tended the flock and for themselves.

---

[17] Francisco, who was a cowboy also looking for new pastures, related this incident to his grandson Hector López.

There was a problem with water for the livestock, so they decided to bring some men from San José to dig a well. They dug the well but found no water. In their plight, Pedro asked advice from a local wise man. He knew there was a wedding the next day at El Guajillo and that his *tocayo*, or namesake, Don Pedrito Jaramillo, would attend.[18] After greeting him, Don Pedrito asked Pedro what he was doing there. Pedro told him the problem they were having finding water where they had settled. Don Pedrito described a nearby lagoon and directed them to ride from the lagoon in a westerly direction until they arrived at a place where deep trails crossed. Near the trails, they would see a mesquite grove, and there they should dig for water.

Pedro left early the next morning to go to El Bordo. There he got the men to start digging close to the mesquite trees. They had been digging a few days when Camilo Palacios put his head close to the wall of the well hole and heard a noise behind the wall. He became curious and hit the spot with the crowbar he used for digging. The water gushed out, widening the hole as it poured through. He became frightened and yelled, "Pull me out, pull me out, I'll drown!" The men, not knowing the depth of the water table, had already dug beneath it, and the water vein, *venero*, poured into the well. This turned out to be a very good well. Using a horse to pull a bucket tied to a rope, they developed the well so it produced plenty of water. They were even able to share the water with their neighbor at El Rancho Solo, with whom they became good friends. Beginning in 1906, Rosendo, Francisco's son, worked as a foreman on the ranch for several years.

Later, Jesús bought 2,500 acres to the north, or the lower section of land from Francisco's El Bordo Ranch near Freer, for 25 cents an acre. His grandchildren remembered an incident that happened to Mauricio, Jesús' son, and Samuel, a son of Mauricio. It seems that while carrying the money to Laredo to pay for the land, they stopped to eat and rest. After resting, they got on their horses and rode off. A few miles down the road, one asked the other, "Do you have the money bag?" When he answered no, they returned as rapidly as they could to where they had rested. Fortunately, no one had come along; the bag of money remained where they had left it.

---

[18] Don Pedrito Jaramillo was a famous healer who came to South Texas in 1881 and lived in Los Olmos near Falfurrias. People throughout the area sought his services. He died in 1907.

The brothers went through many hardships living in the camp. Francisco set up another small *jacal* with a kitchen and brought his oldest daughter, Gumecinda, to do the cooking.

Once, when Rosendo was about nine years old, he was tending a goat herd on horseback. They had some good dogs to help them take care of the herd. Rosendo related to Alejo, his son, an incident involving a rabid full-grown bobcat, *un gato tigerio*. The bobcat approached the flock, and the dogs tried to chase it away. Rosendo moved quickly on his horse to scare away the cat, but the cat came toward his horse instead. Rosendo turned the horse around and rushed toward the camp, calling for help. As he was still calling for help, his sister came out to pull him off the saddle, but his foot got stuck in the stirrup. He could not pull his foot out, so his sister uncinched the saddle and pulled him and the saddle off together. They tried to chase the bobcat away, but it ran into the kitchen. Then Camilo Palacios came to rescue them. He grabbed a hoe with a heavy handle, *azadón de ojo*, and killed the animal. Rosendo recalled that many times they saw mountain lions in the pastures.

Family members would travel back and forth from their camp on El Bordo to San José, where the families stayed. After the drought ended and the pastures of San José had recovered, Pedro and Margarito were the only ones to bring their livestock back to San José. Francisco fixed a permanent residence for himself at his El Bordo Ranch. Jesús remained on his property to the north and improved it. Later he and his family moved near El Bordo to take care of the stock at his ranch there. Rosendo went back to San José to work the fields and cultivate the cotton.

When cotton became a good cash crop, the ranchers concentrated on clearing land for fields. The main tools they used were a mattock, or *talache*, and a good axe, or *hacha*. The people working to clear the land, *desenraiz*, also carried files to keep their tools sharp. The first cotton gin opened at Crestonio or Realitos. The hauling of the cotton bales to the gin took a long time. Later there was a gin in Benavides, a town nearby.

When the railroad came to the area, people from the ranches would go to a ranch called La Palangana to cut wood for the trains. The wood was mainly dried mesquite wood that burned quickly to heat the water to drive the steam engines.

8

A Victim of Rabies

At their open camp near El Bordo, the men set up shades, or *portales*, similar to a lean-to. They slept on the ground under these. The open sides exposed them to the elements as well as to attack by wild animals. One time, an animal bit a man named Ruíz from Rancho San Andrés. He was bitten during the night but did not see the animal. He suspected, however, that it was a skunk and, fearing that it was rabid, went to the ranch house the next day. He told his family what had happened. When he began feeling sick, he asked his relatives to chain him to an old torn-down *sillar* home near the Jesús López house on San Andrés.

Soon he began to show the strong effects of the disease. He began to spit at his relatives and make horrible noises. He would yell and cry very loud as though he was in great pain. His loud cries were reportedly heard all the way back at San José. Someone had been sent to San Antonio for a doctor, but, by the time the doctor arrived, Ruíz was in terrible condition. The doctor told his relatives there was no cure for him, and all that was ahead for him was more suffering. The doctor mixed some medicine for him to drink when he was momentarily calm. The unfortunate man drank the medicine, lay down, and never got up.

9

Pedro and Feliciana López on Rancho San José

Pedro was one of the sons of Antonio López. He married Feliciana Adame, and they raised their family on a portion of Antonio's original Rancho San José. They are remembered by one of their daughters, Ydolina López, who was born December 2, 1895, on the ranch.

Pedro and Feliciana Adame were married on August 31, 1878, in San Diego by Father Peter Bard. Feliciana was born July 9, 1863, in a ranch near Comales, Tamaulipas, a small community south of Camargo. Their ranch property lay close to the Azucar Dam. The house where Feliciana was born was still standing in the 1970s, when members of Pedro López Jr.'s family visited some relatives there. Feliciana's father, Reyes Adame, owned property in Nueces County in the 1870s. Perhaps it was there the couple met.

Pedro López, his daughter Carlota, and his wife, Feliciana Adame, at Rancho San José

To this marriage were born twelve children:

24

Name	Sex	Date of Birth	Married to
Santos López	Female	August 13, 1879	Encarnación Peña
Juanita López	Female	May 16, 1881	Carlos Benavides
Braulia López	Female	May 23, 1883	Daniel Valadez
Victoria López	Female	March 6, 1885	Silverio Valadez
Pedro López	Male	May 5, 1887	Jesusa Valadez
Teresita López	Female	October 15, 1891	Died at age 15
José María López	Male	July 4, 1893	Juanita Oliveira
Ydolina López	Female	December 2, 1895	Praxedis Sáenz
Eduardo López	Male	February 10, 1898	María López
Florentino López	Male	February 8, 1900	Petra García
Carlota López	Female	February 10, 1903	Mateo Valadez
Rafaela López	Female	Unknown	Died at infancy

Pedro and Feliciana also raised a grandson named Raúl Valadez from the age of eight months, when his mother, Braulia, died. Another household member was Santos García, who came to work with Pedro when he was eight years old. He was from Benavides and remained with the family until he married at age twenty-one. Pedro would take him to see his family, hoping he would stay with them. But when it came time to leave, Santos would go back home with Pedro again.

Pedro and Feliciana López built their home near the hand-dug well on San José and planted a palm tree that became a landmark at the site. They lived in a *jacal* at first and later built a wooden frame house with lumber brought from Corpus Christi in the early 1890s. In 1879 Pedro's assets included eight horses valued at $56, twenty sheep valued at $20, ten goats valued at $10, and personal property valued at $15. His brothers Jesús and Francisco also owned taxable property.[19]

From the turn of the century until about 1915, many developments took place at Rancho San José. Members of the family did much work clearing the land and tending the flocks of sheep and goats. Additionally, the family employed many people who brought along their families. They were allowed to live in the *jacales* that were constructed when the family first cleared the land. Survey markers on Antonio's land had the initials "AG," which probably referred to the original grantee, José Antonio González, as this land was part of the La Huerta land grant. A family tale held that a shepherd had stolen the original title papers for the grant from José Antonio González.

---

[19] Tax Assessment Rolls: Nueces County.

Rancho San José as drawn by Ydolina Sáenz in 1980, when she was 85 years old

10

Don Josesito
and Doña Chavela

The house where Antonio and Dominga Peña López lived was still standing in the late 1930s, although there is no sign of it today. José Maldonado, called Josesito, and his wife, Doña Chavela, a couple in their late sixties, lived there. Don Josesito and Doña Chavela were humble people and deeply religious, attending feasts and the Holy Rosary with much devotion. They built an altar in their home, and during Lent the neighbors gathered in their house to pray. The Maldonados had their own prayer rituals, but every Friday they would pray the Rosary and sing hymns of praise, *alabanzas*, for the people of the surrounding area.

Besides his farm work, Don Josesito trained mules for the plow or wagon in order to make a living. Rodolfo, Margarito's grandson, lived across from Don Josesito. One night Don Josesito returned from the grocery store at San José on a donkey, or *burra*, and suffered an injury. Rodolfo recalls that Don Josesito leaned too far to one side to unhook the gate into his yard and fell, breaking his leg. He later died from complications in the hospital in Alice.

The Maldonados often visited Tomás Juan Benavides Jr.'s grandfather's house, always in a joyful mood. Don Josesito continually prayed for rain, good crops, or for someone's health. Tomás, a great-grandson of Pedro López, remembered that he was about six or seven years old when Don Josesito died.

11

Jacales de Leña

The most common type of ranch home was a hut made of logs and brush called a *jacal de leña*. Although the *jacal* was a modest dwelling, its construction required a complex knowledge of local materials and native building techniques.

Ranch hands from Mexico built the *jacales*. They first dug holes for two posts opposite each other and lay mesquite logs between them at about seven feet. The spaces for windows and doors in the *jacales* were left open when laying the logs. Two large center posts with forks at the top supported the roof. A long ridgepole extended from the fork of one vertical post across the length of the *jacal* to the post at the other end. For the first layer of the roof, workers found medium-thick logs and notched them to tie to the ridgepole. After that, smaller-diameter logs were laid crosswise to form the roof. The workers then tied together strips of yucca leaves to make thatching to cover the roof. The leaves came from a South Texas yucca plant called the *pita*. The workers cut strips of the *pita* leaves, or *cortar tiras de oja de pita*. The strips were tied to each other with a special knot that tightened when pulled. After the yucca leaves were in place, workers piled another layer of even thinner branches over them. Then they finished the thatched roof with bundles of grass, called *zacatón*, which they gathered from nearby ponds. Sometimes they used palmetto for this step. They tied the grass bundles together with thin strips of yucca leaves and laid the bundles at the bottom of the roof, working toward the top. After thatching to the top, they next laid bundles lengthwise along the ridgepole to seal the roof crest. They tied the bundles to withstand strong winds, but the roofs still had to be repaired and replaced often.

The *jacales* were used mainly for sleeping. During the winter months, family members filled crevices between the logs with lime mud called *cal*. Stripped cornhusks added fiber to the mortar mix. This porous mix provided a viable insulation that effectively kept the cold wind out. The doors and windows were crudely outlined by straight branches from nearby bushes and trees. A favored tree, the *tenasa*, had straight limbs and was strong and light in weight. The *tenasa* limbs were used for roof slits and to make doors for the *jacales*. At night the crude log doors were lifted and put in place to keep out snakes, skunks, possums, and other small creatures that prowled at night. The *jacales* were made in a variety of sizes and styles, depending on the method preferred by the workers. Some builders spaced the two posts closer and at shorter lengths in order to use split logs.

Workers who followed traditional methods cut the mesquite tree posts, center beams, and the rest of the wood used for making the *jacales* during a full moon. They believed any part of the tree cut during the new crescent-shaped moon retained the sap and so attracted insects, which left a powdery mess that rotted the wood. Houses made of such wood would not last long.

About 1905 Pedro had a large two-room *jacal* for his family, in addition to the wooden frame house he built about 1894. His property probably also included three other *jacales* of different sizes and shapes, where the hired hands and their families lived. People passing through the area who stayed only a day or two before continuing on used the smallest of the *jacales*. These transients helped with the daily chores like cutting wood for the fire, hauling water, and other tasks. The López family fed the visitors and prepared food for them to take when they continued on their journey. The *jacales* were fully occupied during the harvest season. Some of the workers who stayed for an extended time had small children, and Pedro's family became attached to them. They found the visiting children lovable and gracious, and they were sad to see them leave, feeling they had lost part of their own ranch family.

One of the large *jacales* had a fireplace made of stones in a corner for cooking. The *jacales* had a shady porch, a *portal* that was supported by large vertical posts with a Y-shaped fork at the top to support the ridge pole and beams. Crossbeams of smaller diameter covered the first layer of beams, then the thatching of dried cornstalks, *rastrojo*, was laid. The thatching was tied in bundles with yucca leaf strips and secured to the crossbeams. Extra logs were laid over the bundles of *rastrojo* for weight so the wind would not blow off the roof cover. The *portales* provided good shade and protection from the rains for the tables where the family and workers ate.

The people who worked clearing the land were told to save all the mesquite branches and tree trunks for construction materials. They brought in all the straight logs; the crooked logs; the short, middle-sized logs; the thin branches; and the long logs with a Y-shaped end on them. There was a use for each. Windows had no screens, but, in winter, the family made wooden covers for them. Crude wooden doors were placed on front openings in very cold weather.

12

Ranch Houses of *Sillar*

Another type of ranch home was the limestone block house, or *casa de sillar*, peculiar to South Texas. There were two *sillar* houses on Rancho San Andrés, but only one still stood in 1930. A new roof added in the 1940s preserved the building well. The doors faced to the south, the east, and the north, and a window was on the west side that now faces a ranch road. In all probability, a window always faced the road for security reasons.

The last family member to live in this house on Rancho

Sillar *home, San Diego, c. 1908*

San Andrés was Jesús López, the adopted son of Antonio. When Jesús and his family lived there, it had bedrooms built of lumber added to the north and south. The lumber construction was probably board and batten. The kitchen lay to the south and separate from the house as is typical in South Texas ranch homes. The house was occupied in the 1940s.[20]

The other *sillar* house was in ruins in the early 1920s, and no evidence remained by 1990. The *sillares* were probably removed and used

---

[20] Interview with the grandchildren of Jesús López.

Board-and-batten construction, Duval County, c. 1908

for something else. The area where these two houses were located is very rocky. In the late 1930s, eight to ten families lived in the area.

Several other *sillar* houses can be found in the area around San José, La Mota, Guajillo, and Refugio. The entire area is rocky with many caliche pits. These houses were built from limestone blocks about 1820. The houses left standing today lack the gunports that many of the original homes had for protection against the Indians. Two other *sillar* houses still stand on the Hinojosa Ranch, about two miles north of the Gonzalitos Store on Farm to Market Road 1329 going towards San Diego. The *sillar* houses are about a quarter mile away from the road to the west. These two houses had wooden floors and wooden roofs that have now deteriorated. The lumber for these houses was hauled from Corpus Christi.

There were more *sillar* houses located on the Hinojosa Ranch, a large land and livestock enterprise in the area. Antonio Hinojosa Pérez, the oldest son of Luciano Hinojosa and Apolonia Pérez, was born on December 14, 1835, in Agualeguas, Mexico. He came to South Texas about 1850 at age fifteen to work at Las Latas Ranch. After a few years, he became foreman, receiving as part of his wages a herd of sheep and a place to graze them. From this beginning, he started buying parcels of land

and increased his herd of sheep and goats and then added cattle and horses. He bought several thousand acres, which became the Hinojosa Ranch, extending to the El Guajillo community. Mr. Pérez hired many workers and regularly hauled wool and hides to market at Corpus Christi, returning with wagonloads of supplies. He bought more land at Rancho Las Piedritas near Premont. From this ranch, Antonio donated 100 acres to Don Pedrito Jaramillo, who had become a close friend of his. By the time of Antonio's death on November 9, 1912, he had brought all of his relatives from Mexico to share in his fortune. He is buried at El Guajillo Cemetery on land that he owned.[21]

Apparently there were more *sillar* homes northwest of Refugio in the direction of El Guajillo. One house had an eight-foot rock fence around it. The house itself is in ruins, however, and only a part of the wall is left standing. An outline of rocks identifies the area where the fence was situated. The rocks were probably removed and used by the later generations living there. The chimney was the only structure remaining by the 1950s. Because it had a fence for protection, this house may have predated the other ones. It was probably one of the type that had gunports built on it. Indeed, that may be the reason for the name of the town of Refugio, which means refuge.

---

[21] Interview with Tomás Hinojosa of San Antonio, great-grandson of Antonio Hinojosa Pérez.

13

Neighboring Ranches

In the La Mota area, about five miles west of San José, stood more *sillar* homes. In the mid-1930s, members of the Bazán family lived there. These houses were also placed on a rocky hill. The 1870 census lists Rancho Bazán as a landmark as well as Rancho Los Tramojos.

East of Benavides, a few miles out Farm Road 114, a fortlike structure sits on a rocky hill from which the city of Benavides is visible. In the 1940s, this fort had a wooden frame house built on top of it, and a family actually lived there. The ruins of this structure are visible at the side of the road. The fort must have had a very strong roof in order to support a house. If so, it was like other forts with a roof constructed of a limestone mixture called *tipichil*, made from pebbles, sand, lime, and water.

When attacked by the Indians, the ranch families could bolt the downstairs door and climb to the rooms on top to defend themselves. This roof would not catch fire if the Indians shot flaming arrows to burn them out. Tomás Benavides Jr. recalls that his grandfather Pedro López Jr. told him that the stones, *sillares*, used in this fort came from a quarry 100 yards north of the fort.

Another landmark in the area was the Rancho Santa Cruz. Pedro said that, in the mid-1870s when he was close to age eighteen, he worked as a cowboy with his brother Fermán. With some others, they had gone as far south as Rancho Santa Cruz looking for wild horses. They rounded up the horses on the open range around San José. He spoke of the different ranches that were landmarks at the time as they traveled catching horses. Santa Cruz was a thriving community with a store and a school in the 1880s and a post office in the 1920s. A creek that comes from

Concepción in a northeasterly direction runs through Santa Cruz. There was a large lagoon at least a half mile in diameter called El Estero, which always held water. An *estero* is a body of water fed by a river or some other means. Sometimes water comes from underground springs. The lagoon was clogged with heavy growth and vegetation in the center, making it impossible to wade into. The water was always high up to the bank. The area where it emptied into the creek was probably an ideal place to catch wild horses.

In the late 1930s, one could still see two-foot-deep trails coming from different directions to the *estero*. These trails may have been made by animals going to the *estero* or by water running from higher ground. In a field about a half mile northwest of the *estero*, on higher ground, one finds many chips of flint rock. Once in a while after a rain, arrowheads are found. It is possible Indians had camped there and used this waterhole while hunting for meat. The camp area on high ground lay downwind from the *estero*, so the animals would not smell hunting parties lying in wait.

A hand-dug square-shaped well stood about a quarter mile west of the *estero*. Mesquite logs laid in the wall of the well kept the sand from collapsing. This well was perhaps the work of the Benito González family or the Martínez family, who owned this land in the 1860s. The land formed part of the El Señor de la Carrera grant adjudicated to Dionicio Elizondo in 1835. By the 1870s, members of the Elizondo family started selling portions of land, with deeds recorded in the county clerk's office. Sales were made to the Villarreal, Benito González, and Martínez families, who together eventually owned the total 10,096 acres of the grant. The land stayed in one unit until the actual partitions of land were made in the early 1900s, when the owners started fencing their property.

14

Fermán López, Trail Boss on Cattle Drives

Pedro's brother Fermán was in charge of rounding up wild horses, *mesteños*. He and his crew drove the horses to market in San Antonio, Monterrey, Corpus Christi, Mier, and surrounding towns. In those years, the land was open grassland with no fences. Fermán's neighbor Antonio Recio was a tall, strong, robust man skilled as a cowboy. He was dependable and respected in the community. Antonio always wore a six-shooter pistol strapped to his waist and carried a rifle in a scabbard attached to his saddle. Fermán and Antonio Recio were known far and wide for their shooting skills. As they said, "*Donde ponían el ojo ponían la bala,*" which means they were known for their good marksmanship. No one dared engage them in a duel.

Fermán started buying cattle for cattle drives to the stockyards in San Antonio and Houston. He knew all the cattle trails. Because there was no way to haul the cattle and stock to market, the cattle drives provided a means for the area ranchers to sell their livestock. They made a good living at this hard work, considering the low market prices at the time. Fermán bought land with his earnings and even acquired land in the city of San Diego. Pedro also purchased land with his earnings, first at 50 cents an acre, then at $1.00 per acre, later at $2.00 an acre; the last five acres were purchased at $5.00 per acre. It is not known how long Pedro worked with Fermán on the cattle drives. After a few years of the hard drives, they settled down to work their land.

Fermán bought a large amount of land around Rancho El Refugio and Loma Alta. He also owned property in San Diego and many small ranches which people worked for him as sharecroppers. The sharecropper families had children, and, in the bad years of low yields, Fermán personally borrowed money from the bank for their support. He put his own land up as collateral. He helped many people, but over the years Fermán lost most of his land, though he kept enough for his family. He also left horses and city lots in the city of San Diego for them.[22]

A large collection of documents related to Fermán's life shows he once owned 15,000 to 16,000 acres. The documents detail his cattle drives to San Antonio and Houston as well as his other accomplishments. Fermán was the trail boss on the cattle drives and lived a colorful life. On one drive to San Antonio, Fermán met people named López. They were related to him through a sister of his mother, María. The newly found relatives included María Antonia, wife of Bacilio López—Fermán's first cousin.[23]

Fermán's brother Pedro stayed on Rancho San José and occasionally worked as a cowboy at La Chiva, a large ranch owned by brothers Charles and John McNeill. La Chiva comprised 11,000 acres. Some of Pedro's other neighbors also worked there.

---

[22] Information provided by Mrs. Marina López López, a granddaughter of Fermán López.

[23] Information provided by Ricardo González López, a grandson of Fermán López.

15

Planting of Crops in the 1900s

Pedro and Feliciana's daughter Ydolina was six years old when she began helping her brothers Pedro Jr. and José María plant corn and beans in a small field near their house. Pedro plowed a furrow with an ox team, and she followed carrying a small cotton canvas bag strapped over her shoulder. Ydolina counted her steps to space out the kernels of corn. Behind her came José María with another team of oxen dragging an implement that covered the seed. The beans were planted in the same manner. After about a week, the children checked the rows for any plants that did not sprout. They then replanted the empty spaces. Pedro dug a hole with the heavy hoe, *azadón de ojo*, and Ydolina dropped in the seed. Pedro then covered it with his foot. The heavy hoes were used after each rain. It seemed that the weeds always grew faster than the crop.

There was a specific season to plant each crop. Crops had to be planted by a certain date to mature in season. Fortunately, the rains usually came at the right time during the growing season.

16
The Schools around the Year 1900

The ranch families provided for their own education by contributing land, building the schoolhouses, and boarding the teachers at the family's expense. The school on San José was built in the early 1890s. The schools at El Guajillo and La Mota were built later. Most of the students were from seven to fourteen years old.

Charlotte Gunter was the teacher at San José. Everyone called her Carlota. She boarded at the house of Ydolina's grandfather Antonio. Charlotte's hometown was San Antonio, and it was thought that she was related to the owners of the Gunter Hotel. She taught Ydolina songs in English. Ydolina was taken to the other schools for their programs. The schools were close by, so all the neighboring families attended the school programs. Ydolina sang in the school programs at San José, El Guajillo, and La Mota schools. Carlota and Emeterio Peña, a carpenter, were

First schoolhouse on San José, built c. 1890; Pedro López is third from left.

Ydolina's baptismal sponsors, *padrinos de bautizmo*, on November 19, 1896. Miss Gunter maintained a close relationship with Ydolina and over the years gave her gifts.

Eliza Foster was another teacher who later boarded at Antonio's house. Teachers who taught at San José in later years were:

- María López, a daughter to Margarito López, who later married Margarito Bazán from La Mota
- Zela Foster, who may have been related to Eliza Foster
- Santos Bazán Cantú
- Belia García
- Juanita Oliveira from Benavides, who married José María López
- Rebecca Elizalde
- Pajita García.

Some of these teachers rotated between the three schools. Ydolina attended school for about six years, but she only went to school about three or four months each year because of a tumor in her head. She had constant headaches, and her eyes swelled. Over the years, she completed the third grade and started the fourth grade. She and her cousin Amadeo helped the teacher with the first graders.

In the 1919 storm, the schoolhouse at San José was lifted from its foundation and swept about fifty feet west of its original location. Community members repaired the school and set it on a new foundation of pylons, *pilones*, near the new place where it had landed. In 1925 a new, larger schoolhouse was built. The old school continued in use as a voting place, a *casilla*, for precinct elections until another place was designated.

17

Padre Pedro

Father Peter Bard, a Catholic priest, came through San José about once a month. The locals at San José called him Padre Pedro. He arrived in late afternoon after visiting with the people in the ranches close to the road. On his arrival, he rang the school bell and greeted the people. The people from the surrounding ranches then came for the Rosary and to sing hymns of praise, *cantos* or *alabanzas*. Padre Pedro spoke and sang to them in Spanish and told them to bring forward the children to be baptized. He explained the church teachings, the *doctrina*, and the sacraments and commandments, the *sacramentos y mandamientos*.

Ydolina said, "In his talks, he gave very wise advice to both old and young." "*Daba consejos muy sabios a grandes y chicos en sus pláticas.*" He also visited the sick, prayed for them, and gave them encouragement, *mucho ánimo*, making them feel better. Through his teaching, there was much love and respect among people, "*había mucho cariño y respeto entre la gente.*" The older people were called uncles and aunts, or *tios y tias*, and the older cousins were called brothers and sisters, *hermanos y hermanas*. The older people who belonged to the community were addressed with titles of respect, *don or doña*.

The morning after Padre Pedro's arrival, the school bell rang, and the neighbors came before breakfast to attend mass. Ydolina's mother, Feliciana, got up early to make breakfast for the Padrecito and fix food for him to eat as he traveled. Padre Pedro said that Pedro and Feliciana were the first couple he married when he came to San Diego. After the new school was built, the old school continued in use for services when Padre Pedro visited.

18

Constructing Wells on the Ranch

One of the most pressing needs on the ranch was obtaining fresh drinking water. About 1904 Pedro and his family hand-dug a fourth well about three-quarters of a mile west of San José. Pedro hired help to tend his flock, to clear the land, and to help dig the wells. The fourth well, about 45 feet deep, had a bell shape at the bottom of the shaft. A round pool rose in the middle, surrounded by a raised ledge. Family members who dug the well said that, from the bottom, one could see the stars during the day. One night, as the well was being finished, water broke through the well wall and rose to 35 feet. All the digging tools had been left inside the well for the night, and no one wanted to go underwater to retrieve them, so the tools remained at the bottom of the well.

Elderly people in the area remembered the hand-digging of the wells. The ones on San José are round, from eight to ten feet in diameter, providing enough space for two people to work inside at a time. It was best for them to work in pairs, so if something happened to one of the diggers, the other could secure him to the rope to be pulled out. Fortunately, at San José there was no loose sand that could cause the walls to cave in.

The family used various methods to determine where to dig. Some people used a Y-shaped peach tree twig to locate water. When Pedro dug his first well, Don Pedrito Jaramillo, the healer from Los Olmos near Falfurrias, told him the direction and approximate distance from his house to go. He told Pedro to bury a tin can upside down and to check it the next day; if there was moisture inside, he should dig his well there.

Don Pedrito Jaramillo, healer

The well-digging implements included a mattock, or *talache*; picks; shovels called *palas*; and metal crowbars. The crowbars had a wide, flattened cutting edge on one side and a sharp-pointed edge on the other side for cutting into the white limestone on each side of the well. The workers set two heavy, forked posts upright to secure the crossbeam that held the pulley. The pulley lowered the men into the hole and lifted them out. It was also used to lower the tools and take out the buckets of dirt. In the San José area, they did not dig very deep before they struck the white limestone layer, so most of these wells are solid rock from top to bottom. The men chipped the rock and shoveled it into a large cowhide container secured with ropes at the four corners. A heavy rope at a central point on the cowhide threaded through a pulley that was attached to the crossbeam over the well opening. A man leading a mule raised and lowered the load on the rope.

There was discussion about whether the ideal time to dig a well was winter or summer. In fact, it did not matter once the hole was deeper than ten feet. At that depth, the surrounding dirt was cool in the summer and warm in winter. The many stories about the challenges of digging wells reveal the hardships and hard work that the people faced to survive. But water was a basic necessity on the ranch, and the wells they dug provided good water.

Another structure that helped provide water for the ranch was the man-made earthen dam, or *presa*, along one of the many stream beds, or *arroyos*. An earthen dam was built near the last deep well Pedro dug. When the family worked the field about three-quarters of a mile west of San José, they passed near this *presa*. When digging the well, workers used dirt from the well hole to build a levy on the east and west side. They used the rest of the dirt to block the passage of a creek to divert the flow of water to the reservoir. This *presa* always had water for the cattle in times of drought, and it had fish when it was flooded from an upstream body of water. Pedro made fish hooks for the family out of wire, and, on the way back home in the afternoon, they fished and took home the catch to be prepared for a meal.

When the heavy rains came, the *presa* overflowed on the west side. The creek continued on its way, taking some of the fish through the *arroyo* down to Rufino Vela's and Margarito's properties. Mr. Vela and Margarito had also dug some round holes, *tinajas*, beside the creek to divert some of the floodwater. These *tinajas* held water for their cattle and trapped fish that followed the currents. When the holes were half full of water, the people gathered the fish in burlap sacks, carried them in buckets and tubs to the *presa*, and threw them in.

Around the 1930s, these creeks still held water year-round, but the water had become stagnant. It developed yellow foam, called *lama,* on the surface, which was thought to come from the leaves of the tall trees that grew beside the creeks. Some lagoons retained water for a

Rufino and María Lira de Vela on their ranch in Duval County, c. 1910

long time after a rain—those at lower elevations were fed by water running in gullies or ravines from the higher ground. By 1950 all these creeks had dried up.

19

Raising Cotton

By 1905, with provisions for water and livestock made, the family directed their energy toward production of cotton as a cash crop. Cotton became a leading crop as land was cleared for tillable fields. Pedro Jr., José María, and Ydolina worked the fields. Raising cotton entailed a lot of work. They weeded with heavy hoes in a process called *despajar*, then thinned in a process called *desahijar*, and cleaned out the fields again after each rain. Finally came the picking of the cotton balls.

In the early years, the family members used oxcarts to go to the fields. Later, they traveled in a mule-drawn wagon called a *guajín*. To haul the cotton, they used large, heavy, mule-drawn wagons with high sideboards as skirts. These skirts held a bale of cotton weighing about 1,500 pounds. The family hauled the bales to Calvin North's cotton gin in Benavides. The roads and wagon trails had rocks, bumps, and sand, so the wagons required at least two or three teams of mules to pull the load. About 1920 area ranchers were raising cotton because it provided instant cash on the favorable market.

The family profited from their industry. Pedro continued to buy land from 1910 through 1915. These were profitable years. Ydolina as the family bookkeeper and treasurer recorded the revenue from cotton sales, the sale of livestock, and payment to workers on the ranch. Every member of the family had chores to do. The older daughters who were not married helped with the cooking, washing, or tending the garden. When not working in the fields, Pedro Jr. continued clearing the land and digging new water wells. In later years Florentino and Eduardo worked in the fields when school was not in session. José María tended sheep when there were no other young men among the hired hands to do the work. When shepherds were available, he worked alongside Pedro Jr.

20
Tick Fever

Pedro constructed some corrals with lumber given him by the McNeill brothers, which he hauled to his ranch in the mule-drawn wagon. He built one corral on San José and another on land he owned northwest of San José. These corrals came in handy in 1933, when a severe tick fever epidemic hit the area. The cattle were quarantined and could not be taken in or out of the area. Mr. Jiménez, a mason, or *albañil*, constructed a dipping vat close to the corral northwest of San José. Jiménez also built a concrete water trough at the *presa*.

For a couple of months, the cattle had to be dipped every seven days, then every fourteen days, and finally every twenty-one days. The tick inspectors supervised the herd being treated in the vats. At one end of the vat, a slippery slope caused the cattle to fall into the deep end of the long trough and became completely immersed in the medicinal mix. Then they swam for a few feet to the other end of the trough, where the concrete rose gradually to ground level. The up-slope of the trough had ridges so the cattle did not slip getting to the drying pen, and the drying pen had a sloped floor that allowed the medicine to drain back into the vat, thus conserving the medicine. Before the cattle were released from the drying pen, workers marked them on the rump with green paint indicating that the cow had been treated for the week.

The tick inspectors monitored all movement of livestock within the quarantined area of the county. They also periodically checked the medicine in the vat to confirm its strength. When young calves were dipped, they were hooked under the neck with a bent rod to pull them to the vat. Horses had to be dipped also. During this tick fever epidemic, men on horseback drove the livestock from surrounding ranches to a dipping vat and then took them back to pasture. The tick inspectors were Sabas de los Santos in Benavides, Margarito Bazán in the San José area, Mateo Valadez in La Bandera, and José María Sáenz in the Mesquite Bonito area.

21

Dog Protection at Night

At night the dogs provided protection against the wild animals. Pedro was a light sleeper and recognized the various ways the dogs barked. He could detect when they were being attacked by a vicious animal or just barking a warning to keep away prowling animals. He kept his rifle ready near his bed. Sometimes the dogs barked at coyotes that tried to get into the sheep and goat pens, and Pedro fired his gun to scare the coyotes away. Some of the people passing through on wagons, or *carretelas*, wanted to stay for the night. They slept in their wagons during the summer to be safe from prowling animals.

22

Shopping Trips to Town

Pedro's ranch was the central location where the family sheared the sheep. The shearers gathered the wool into small burlap sacks. When these were full, they packed the sacks into a larger burlap sack that held about 100 pounds. During the early 1880s, the burlap sacks were loaded onto two-wheeled carts pulled by oxen and hauled to Corpus Christi. Usually two people made the trip. The family also took animal hides to sell on these trips.

On these early trips to Corpus Christi, Pedro took along his father-in-law, Reyes Adame, or his brother-in-law, Ponciano. In later years, the sacks of wool were loaded into mule-drawn wagons that had wooden bows on top with a tarpaulin tied over them to protect the wool from rain.

Many preparations were needed for the trips to market in Corpus Christi. A trip either by oxcart or mule-drawn wagon would take six to seven days. First the family prepared food for the trip. A favorite was *panochitas* made from dough of cornmeal, sugar, lard, and cinnamon tea. The women squeezed handfuls of dough and laid them in a pan to bake. These could be eaten with a meal or for snacks. Another favorite was bread called *pan flojo*, similar to the present-day bread baked outdoors and made with either flour or cornmeal, *pan de campo*. The travelers also packed dried jerky meat called *carne seca*, as well as coffee, sugar, salt, spices, cooking utensils, tin cups for coffee, a jug of water, and other personal things. They carried a gun to hunt fresh meat such as rabbits or wild turkeys and to protect against wild or rabid animals. Sometimes neighboring ranch people accompanied them, also hauling wool to Corpus Christi.

On the way back, the travelers brought lumber, hardware supplies, farm and ranch tools, and grocery staples. They purchased lard in 24-pound cans called *arrobas de manteca gringa,* which they used in making flour tortillas. They brought sacks of sugar, beans, potatoes, coffee, rice, and vermicelli. Feliciana ordered piece goods in 20-, 30-, or 50-yard bolts of different colored flannel called *felpa,* as well as bleached and unbleached muslin. She sewed the unbleached muslin into summer underwear, kitchen curtains, and room dividers. The bleached muslin, a finer weave of cloth, was used for linens, shirts, and their finest underwear.

All the women in the family learned to sew the different kinds of cloth and garments. Santos, Juanita, Braulia, Victoria, and Ydolina by age fourteen sewed and made the clothing for the family. Ydolina sewed the long johns, *calzoncillos largos* that reached to the ankles. She made six buttonholes opposite each other and sewed very thin strips of cloth as strings to lace through the holes and tie together at the ankles. She also made buttonholes at the waist so it could be laced; there was no elastic at the time. Later, snap buttons were used. Ydolina fashioned men's tops like today's tee shirts with a V-neck. These undershirts had longer sleeves for the older men. For very special occasions, she made shirts of fine bleached muslin for her brothers. She also constructed women's underwear, petticoats, blouses, and simple dresses of gray, navy blue, black, or brown fabric with white collars. On some of the dresses, she trimmed the collars and sleeves with crocheted lace.

Ydolina

The men bought good durable shoes for the family on trips to Corpus Christi. Mostly they limited their purchases to work shoes, but occasionally they bought dress shoes. They usually guessed at the sizes, and only rarely did the shoes fit right. The wrong-size shoes were exchanged on the next trip weeks later. Another item they had to buy was pants. Pants were made of a material similar to present-day denim called *mesclía*. The work pants were available in dark colors only—blue, black, or gray.

There may have been commercial dyes available, but, in the 1880s, the family boiled the roots of plants to color the unbleached cloth for living room curtains. They used the root of the *agarito* plant to dye the cloth a yellow color and the root of an oak tree, the *chaparro prieto*, for a dark purplish color. After 1920 calico prints became available in different types of cloth.

On these trips hauling the wool to Corpus Christi, the family had to rely on good weather and hope there were no flooded road sections. They knew all the roads that passed close to low areas or lagoons. They planned how long they would travel each day, noting where it would be safe to sleep and where to water and feed the animals. They selected sleeping places close to a ranch they knew from previous trips.

23

Old Types of Beds and Bedding

In the past, the family slept on beds made of hand-hewn boards and posts. The builder first nailed four horizontal boards to four vertical posts, then placed smaller boards across the top to hold the mattress. Sometimes the family nailed a cowhide to the boards to help hold the mattress. This type of bed was a platform bed called a *tarima*. To make a mattress, the women washed cornshucks, then shredded them with a fork and stuffed them as filling into a heavy canvas material called mattress ticking. In rare cases, they filled some mattresses with a type of dry grass. Later, when the family began raising cotton, they gathered residue left in the fields after the cotton crop had been picked. The pillows were made of the same fabric and filled with the same materials. These were times of poverty and hard work. A tired body could rest and sleep almost anywhere.

In the early 1920s, when Pedro stopped raising sheep and began raising beef cattle, he saved the wool from the few sheep he had left. Women washed the wool in a lagoon with soap to remove the oil, then carded it for use in making quilts and pillows. Sometimes the mattresses were filled with a mixture of cotton and wool. Some blankets were bought ready-made from peddlers or buyers who bartered for the animal hides. One of the peddlers who came to the ranches was from the Alfredo Santos firm in Laredo.

Sheep and goat skins were dried and cured and used as sleeping pads. At times the family would throw the smaller hides on the floor for the youngest children to sleep on. At other times these skins, *cueros*, were

A peddler on his rounds in Duval County, c. 1908

used like today's rubber sheets, so the babies would not wet the bedding or mattress.

Larger cowhides were spread out to dry and then salted and cured for making chaps. Strips were cut from the hide wide enough to make mule harnesses. Rawhide reins and ropes were braided. Reyes Adame, Ydolina's maternal grandfather, cut very thin strips of these hides. Using an awl, he made holes in the leather and used strips as backing to repair shoes, harnesses, and saddle bags. He also made leather bags to carry in the buggies.

The women of the house were creative in using the resources available to them on the ranch. They made quilts in simple designs from scrap pieces of material. They covered old blankets with flannel and wove rugs out of rags and leftover fabric scraps.

24

Making Soap and Washing Clothing

Although soap was available in larger cities, ranch families made most of their own soap. They took the tallow from the barrels and boiled it again, then added lye and lime. In some cases, rose petals were thrown in for fragrance. They poured the liquid onto a flat surface to cool, dry, and harden. When it was hard, they cut the sheet of soap into square bars. This soap had a yellowish color and was used to wash clothing.

They washed clothes in a lagoon about a half mile south of San José, near the second water well behind Margarito's house. The women loaded the dirty clothes in sacks and large tubs and hauled them in the mule-drawn wagon to the lagoon. In later years, the clothes were hauled to the lagoon in a buckboard. The women brought along a large iron kettle, a *cazo*, and a 1" x 12" board for kneeling on at the edge of the water. It took at least two people to do the washing.

Most of the clothing was work clothing, which was soaked in large pots of water boiling over a fire to remove the sweat, dirt, and grime. The women shaved the homemade soap into the hot water to dissolve before adding the clothes. After boiling the clothes, they knelt on a board at the water's edge and rinsed the wash in the lagoon. White linens they soaked in a bluing solution, then rinsed. They spread the clothing to dry on nearby trees, shrubs, and bushes. At first, Santos, the oldest daughter, and Victoria did the washing.

Later, Braulia, Juanita, and Ydolina did it. If the clothing was not completely dry, the women brought it back in a tub for drying at home. Still later, they did the washing at home in a tub with a washboard.

During the summer, they bathed some of the small children near the water troughs, *canoas*, with a tin cup, or *moca*. The bathing soap was similar to present-day crystal white soap, called *jabón del borrego*. The older family members and children washed inside the *jacales* in a large tub, pouring water from a bucket. They also used the *moca* and *jabón del borrego*. During the cold winter, a fire was built inside the *jacal* to heat the water for bathing.

25

Slaughtering a Hog

When one of the large, fat hogs was killed, all the relatives were called to help because everything had to be done the same day. If the family wanted to slaughter a hog, they would separate one from the rest of the herd and put it in a separate pen. This hog was fed corn and mesquite beans to fatten it for slaughter. The other hogs were fed scraps from the kitchen. They also were fed pigweed, or *quelite*, a wild plant that grows during the rainy season. During the months of May and June, the family fed the hogs other types of feed, such as prickly pears. To collect them, Pedro would take some members of his family in the mule-drawn wagon to the rocky hills east of San José. There the family gathered prickly pear tunas for the hogs. There were large cactus patches, *nopaleras*, past San Andrés near La Muralla Ranch.

After killing the hog, they proceeded with the removal of the hair from the skin. To do this, they filled big pots with hot water in which to dip the carcass and moisten the hair, then they scraped the skin with sharp knives to shave off the hair. The skin was washed again with soapy water. Finally, the workers cut the carcass open to get at the meat.

After trimming off all the fat, they cut the meat into strips and hung it up. The fat chunks cut from the meat were put into a large iron pot, a *paila*, to cook on an outside fire, while the cuts of meat were fried with the rinds in their own fat on another fire. After the grease dripped from the meat and rinds, the pieces were laid on a screen to dry. The fried rinds were cracklings, or *chicharrones de cuero*.

The cubed, bite-size pieces of meat and fat were also fried and then placed in a burlap sack. To squeeze out the fat, two people twisted a

Slaughtering a hog,
Atascosa County, 1901

stick at each end of the sack in opposite directions. These pieces, called *chicharrones de carne*, were also placed on a screen to drip dry.

Some pieces of the choice meat were ground to make the sausage, *chorizo*, preserved with spices, *chile colorado*, and vinegar. The intestines, called *las tripas*, were cleaned to use as casing and stuffed with the ground meat. Some strips were cut to form the sausage links. The *chicharrones de carne* were served with eggs for breakfast, cooked just plain and eaten with corn tortillas or bread, or cooked with beans. The *chicharrones* kept for some time. Finally, the family made *tamales* from the choice ground meat.

Much care was taken when frying to ensure that the meat did not burn or brown too much or ruin the fat. The fat left in the *paila* was strained through a fine cloth to make sure no meat was left to spoil. They poured the whitest fat into cans to save for cooking later. The fat remaining was put into wooden barrels to use as tallow, *manteca o cebo*, for making soap.

26

Food Preparation

Some cooking was done in a large *jacal* with a fireplace in one corner. An opening in the top allowed the smoke to escape. Cooking implements included black cast iron pots (*ollas*), grills (*parrillas*), and large griddle plates (*comales*) to cook the corn or flour tortillas. When cooking, the women moved the coals to one side to keep coffee and other food warm. Corn was boiled in a lime solution to make the corn dough, the *nixtamal*, for the corn tortillas. For the main meals, the women boiled the rice, beans, and other foods, such as cowboy stew (*carne guisada*), ground meat, hash (*picadillo*), or jerky stew (*caldillo con carne seca*).

The meat usually came from a sheep, goat, calf, or small hog. Some animal was usually killed daily, since venison, wild turkey, rabbit, quail, and other kinds of wild meat were plentiful. When there were not many people eating, the leftover meat was shared with brothers and sisters who lived nearby.

Before refrigeration ranch people had to dry their meat, since all of it was not consumed in one day. Women sliced the leftover meat into thin layers to dry. They cut the layers of meat into small pieces and placed them over a wire line similar to a clothesline. They hung the lines high so the dogs could not reach them. To ensure even drying, they salted the strips of meat and spread them with a wooden stick. After a few days in the hot sun and the wind, the meat pieces were ready to continue air drying in burlap sacks. People hung the sacks from the top beam inside the *jacales*. Someone would place a round piece of tin with a hole in the middle around the rope to keep the rats or mice from sliding down to get to the meat. Axle grease was smeared on the wire to keep the ants away. In the kitchen, shorter lines, called *sarsos*, held smaller amounts of meat or stored food. *Sarsos* too had axle grease on the wire ends and the round tin protectors. When meat was needed, family members pounded the burlap sacks with something heavy to make it soft for cooking and eating, creating what we know as beef jerky. They cooked delicious-tasting soups, *caldillo*, with the strips of meat and potatoes, spices, and vermicelli, or *fideo*.

In addition to keeping major herds of sheep, goats, and cattle, the ranch family raised poultry. The hens provided eggs for breakfast, although some eggs were saved to hatch chickens. When the chickens were grown, they were eaten also. Caring for the chickens required feeding them corn, cooping them up at night, and turning them out in the day.

Most of the ranches had goats, and they were milked in the evening. The milk was boiled before drinking. Shepherds took sheep and goats out to the pasture during the day and brought them in at night, putting them in the corrals.

27

Use of Corn

For lunch and supper, the cooks used onions, garlic, and vegetables from the garden when in season. In the traditional Mexican diet, corn was basic. The families ate fresh corn on the cob, *elote*, when in season, or corn cooked in various ways, as well as squash. Beans and cornbread, called *pan de maíz* or *pan de campo*, were a regular part of the meals. They made some of the scraped corn into *tamales, tamales de elote*. For dessert they roasted the cornmeal and mixed it with milk, sugar, and ground cinnamon to make a pudding called *pinole*. Another mixture was squeezed into cookies, *panochitas de elote*. These could be eaten as a snack or as a dessert after meals. The *panochitas de elote* kept for a long time and were handy on trips, although they were so tasty that they didn't last long. The women could never make enough of them! On birthdays they baked cakes from scratch and made jams, jellies, and fillings or toppings for the cakes.

The men harvested the rows of cornstalks, cutting them with a machete. They brought the corn harvest from the fields in a mule-drawn wagon and stored it in a corncrib, a *chapil*. The *chapiles* were like the crude *jacales*, except the roofs resembled those of the *portales* to protect the corn from the sun, weather, and rain. The *chapiles* provided long-term storage for the ears of corn, *mazorcas de maíz*.

When ready to use it, the family shelled the corn and placed it in burlap sacks. They washed the husks and saved them for wrapping *tamales* or shredded them later for use as mattress filling or to be mixed in the mortar for the walls of the *jacales*. They shelled the corn by putting the husked ear into a corn sheller, a *desgranadora de maíz*, which was secured to a three- to four-foot-square wooden box, where the kernels of corn were collected. Someone turned the handle on the corn sheller, while someone else fed the ears into it. The family then poured the kernels of corn into cotton sacks, loaded them onto the mule-drawn wagon, and hauled them to the Moses Ranch about seven miles east of San José, where the kernels were ground into cornmeal. With the cornmeal, family members made cornbread; *tamales*; cookies, or *panochitas*; roasted cornmeal, or *pinole*; and other desserts.[24]

When beans were ready for harvest, the family pulled them out of the ground, turned them upside down to dry, gathered them together, and placed them inside a sack. They beat the sack with a stick to break the beans out of the pods, then poured them into a bucket. They lifted the bucket of beans to head height and poured them slowly into a washtub, while a cross wind blew out the chaff. They did this at least twice before they placed the beans in burlap sacks and stored them in the *jacales*.

[24] The Moses Ranch along the road from Gonzalitos to Highway 281 had modernized buildings.

28

Wild Plants Used at San José

Living in the country, ranch families became familiar with a variety of plants and trees, many of which were peculiar to South Texas. They used some of the plants to feed the livestock and others for human consumption or medicinal purposes. A *coma* tree produced a green berry. When it ripened, the berry juice oozed out and hardened on the outside. It tasted like gum, *chicle*, when chewed. The ranch families also gathered red berries, *pitahayas*, from the barrel cactus, the *viznaga*. These particular plants grew in the fields and produced three-inch white, carrotlike roots that were washed, peeled, and eaten raw. They tasted sweet and nutty. During the spring planting, the children followed in the plowed furrows and collected these roots, called *chancaquillas*, putting them in jars or bags.

Another plant, the *agarita*, had a red berry that ripened about Easter time. The berries were collected and boiled with sugar until thickened, producing a very tasty tart jelly. A plant with medicinal value was *salvia*, or sage. Prepared as a tea, it helped babies fight diarrhea and nursing mothers produce milk.

Lemon balm, or *toronjíl*, is another plant that grows wild near San José but only where there is lime, or caliche, in the soil. It blooms in the spring and has a lemonlike scent that makes it easily identifiable among other plants in the pasture. This small plant is cut and boiled to make a tea. To make the tea, it is best to bring the water to a boil, then lower the heat to steep until it is as strong as desired and sweeten with sugar or honey. This tea has a soothing effect and helps people sleep. It does not induce sleep but lets one relax so that sleep comes more easily. If taken before meals in a strong concentrated essence, it helps digestion and prevents stomach gas when a person eats too much fried food. Fruits also grew on the ranch: oranges; peaches; bananas; pomegranates, or *granados*; and figs. At the front of the house, Pedro liked plants and flowers such as roses, jasmine, and honeysuckle, or *madreselva*. He also grew medicinal herbs such as sweet basil, or *albacar*; mint, or *yerba buena*; a bitter-leafed plant called rue, or *ruda*; rosemary, or *romero*; and wormseed, or *estafiate*.

Another useful plant was a popular one in Mexico, the century plant, often called *maguey* by people of that area. Feliciana's father, Reyes Adame, lived with the family on the ranch until 1920. He walked west of San José through an old creek bed to gather some American agave, or *maguey*. He cut some of the prickly leaves, *pencas*. After cutting off the thorns, he carried the leaves on his back to the ranch. He then dug a hole in the ground to bury the leaves, separating each leaf with rocks. He covered the hole with dirt and piled red-hot coals on top. When the fire died out and the *maguey* leaves had cooled, Reyes washed them, peeled the skin, and cut them into small pieces, saving only the small tender leaves. This tasted like cactus jelly.

Reyes also made the traditional Mexican beer, *pulque*, from which tequila is distilled. To make the *pulque*, he cut a hole or a pit into the center of the *maguey* plant and covered it with dirt. He took the piece cut from the center and wrapped it to protect it from the dirt. He cooked it with the rest of the plant in the ashes and coals. After cooking, it formed a jelly or caramel, *cajeta*. The next morning, Reyes uncovered the pit he had dug into the center of the *maguey* and dipped out a white milky substance that had seeped into the hole. After fermenting, the liquid was called *pulque* and had a liquor smell. Reyes liked to drink the *pulque* at midmorning between breakfast and lunch. The cooked center part of the plant was prepared with sugar, cinnamon, or aniseed (*anís*) to enhance its taste as an excellent dessert.

Reyes was born and reared near the Azucar Dam in the Comales area in Mexico. He may have learned these customs from his parents or relatives. No one else at San José knew these recipes, although there were plenty of yuccas, *pitas*, in the pastures. Reyes knew when the center flowery bloom ripened and was ready to eat and not be bitter. He would cut the flowery center and trim off the outer parts to eat raw like a salad or boil as a steamed vegetable. The stalk was fed to the pigs.

29

Horseback Racing and Music

Pedro had a keen interest in racehorses from 1910 until about 1918. He acquired some racehorses and built some tracks, *veredas*, to train his horses. Later, he opened the tracks for racing on weekends. The racing tracks ran east and west on a tract of land southwest of San José. At the time, many of the ranchers were making the transition from sheep to cattle ranching and owned horse herds. Cowboys came from the surrounding areas of El Guajillo, La Esperanza, La Bandera, Palito Blanco, Mesquite Bonito, and even Benavides. The races usually were held on Sundays during the late spring and summer. They were an exciting social event that brought people together for a break from all the hard work.

Pedro was a slender person and not too tall. At times he would race his own horses. Triunfo Treviño, a young man from Rancho Bretaña, trained and ran his horses as well.

At the races, each rancher would place a wager against another person. Bets were made in *reales*, or bits. A bit was worth about 12½ cents, so *dos reales* equaled 25 cents, four *reales* was 50 cents, 12 *reales* was $1.50, and 14 *reales* was $1.75. Few bets were over a dollar. Fifty-cent bets were the most common. Most jockeys raced bareback, although occasionally someone would use a wide leather band to strap himself onto his horse. The cowboys loved their horses and had confidence in them, and that made for lots of fierce competition.

The last horse Pedro raced was named El Indio. After the horses passed the finish line, *la raya*, the jockeys started pulling the reins to slow the horses. Suddenly one of the reins on Pedro's horse broke. The horse could not be controlled with one rein and ran off toward the pasture at

Pedro López on El Indio with his brother Fermán holding the reins

the end of the cleared area. Pedro escaped serious injury only by dodging tree branches until the horse stopped. After this narrow escape, Pedro decided it was time to quit racing.

At about this time, a rare incident of violence occurred. Eduardo and Florentino had started playing the guitar and violin at the horse races, at small gatherings, and family celebrations. The dances at that time took place at the school or in family living rooms. At one of the celebrations, a dance area had been cleared. A person named García made a profane remark about their father, Pedro. Eduardo heard it and got into a heated discussion with the man. In the dispute, Eduardo used his violin as a weapon. That ended the argument and the dance.

Pedro was a law officer in his precinct. Mr. Librado de la Garza, a deputy sheriff from San Diego, appointed Pedro to go with him at times to serve legal papers on people in the area.

30

An Homage to Don Yrineo Salinas

About 1902 a man named Yrineo Salinas lived on Francisco's ranch at San Andrés. Don Yrineo was recognized by all as a pious man of prayer who always talked to others about God and giving thanks. He was the one to pray during times of drought and sickness. When he was old and nearing his last days, he told everyone that, on the day he died, there would be heavy rains.

Alejo López's father, Rosendo, remembered a marker dated 1902 at the back of their fields, where Don Yrineo was buried in a shallow grave. He was buried in such a grave because it rained for two days and nights after he died. Anyplace the grave diggers tried to dig became mud. Alejo said his mother, Lucia, had a lot of faith in this man. During droughts the family would go to his grave and pray. Within three days, they would get a rain. This devotion lasted for a generation, until about 1920. After that, no more processions occurred or devotions took place.

31

La Voz del Cielo

Family members related many spiritual and religious stories. Pedro often received special messages that the family referred to as a voice from heaven, *la voz del cielo*. One cold winter night, when freezing sleet was falling, Pedro received a message. He borrowed Feliciana's heavy hose and put on two pairs of pants, a heavy coat, and a raincoat. He also asked for a heavy coat and some blankets to take in his wagon. He hitched his mule and drove to a ranch near San Diego, where a young child was very sick. He took the young girl and her parents to Alice to see a doctor. The child had pneumonia and would have died if Pedro had not reacted so quickly. Many years later, the young girl and her family visited the López family, remembering that Pedro had saved her life.

Pedro sometimes received messages from people who had passed away. Some messages advised Pedro to remind a certain individual about a mass that had been promised but not yet celebrated. He received other messages foretelling of danger to people he was to warn.

When Ydolina was about eight years old, she experienced a strange sensation. She felt the presence of a large animal climbing into her bed as she slept. She said she felt it curling up like a big cat, such as a panther. Ydolina exchanged sides in the bed with her sister and even went to sleep in another room, but the presence followed her there also. Many times her father slept inside the doorway of the room with a rifle, but Ydolina still felt the presence. She was scared and cried. This problem lasted until the family made a trip to Don Pedrito Jaramillo. Through his prayers, Ydolina was left at peace. After that, very few things frightened her.

32

Young Boys Taken by the Indians

The older members of the family told stories about Indians in South Texas. Feliciana Adame López, called "Mamá Chana" by her great-grandson Tomás Juan Benavides Jr., remembered when the Indians used to pass by the ranch on their migrations. In the fall they passed going south, and in the spring they returned going north. On one of these migrations, between 1879 and 1885, the Indians found a young boy about six or seven years old playing in the pasture, and they took him with them. The young boy was from a ranch near the cemetery. The boy lived with the Indians for several years. Every time the Indians passed his home, he would tell them, "That is where my parents live."

One time, when he was fourteen or fifteen years old, as they passed by the ranch, he stopped and returned to his family. "Mamá Chana" said the young man refused to wear shoes, even when it was cold. He did not like to wear pants or a shirt, preferring instead to wear a loincloth. Everyone was greatly impressed that he could lay a handkerchief on the ground, walk around the house, shoot an arrow over the house, and hit the handkerchief with the arrow.

"Mamá Chana" also said Felix Sáenz, a ten-year-old boy from Rancho El Guajillo, was taken by the Indians too. Felix escaped when he was about twenty years old by lying underwater and breathing through a cane until it was dark.

67

33

El Gaujillo Community

El Guajillo was a thriving community in the 1900s, predating even San José. It had a post office in a small store, a *tendajito*, and later a gas station. Gabriel Ramírez owned the store and was postmaster. Isidoro Benavides carried the mail on horseback from San Diego to El Guajillo, working for a year without pay to help establish the post office. Later, when a mail route was established, Enrique García delivered mail from a Model A Ford.[25]

Early truck, San Diego, c. 1908

---

[25] Information provided by Tomás Hinojosa of San Antonio, who was born and raised in El Guajillo.

34

Continued Development at San José

About 1916 Silverio Valadez and his relative Martín Valadez owned a store on Rancho San José. They developed a good business, but their success was short-lived. During World War I, both were drafted into the service. The store changed hands and was passed to José María, Ydolina, and Pedro to run. Because of wartime rationing, they could sell only one or two pounds of some staple groceries like sugar to each family per week. It became difficult to deal with some customers because they could not understand the reasons for the rationing and got upset. Finally, the Lópezes decided to close the store. They felt that it was not worth making enemies, including some of their relatives, over something they could not remedy.

The storm of 1919 did not damage the store building. The following year, Pedro López Jr., his wife, Jesusa, and family moved from La Bandera into the store building. They had to remove some shelving to make the rooms more livable.

In 1925 a new, larger school was built on San José. It stood near the road leading into San Diego from the ranches south of San José. The carpenter for the school was Mr. Bazán, and his helpers were Encarnación Peña and Pedro López Jr. Natalia Sáenz López was the first teacher in the school, from 1926 to 1927. She boarded at José María and Juanita Oliveira López's. The next year Natalia taught at El Guajillo.

The López family hired Mr. Gil Hinojosa from Benavides to drill a water well for them in 1926. This well had a windmill and cistern. In the early 1920s, there was a blacksmith shop near Rancho El Saltillero ran by blacksmith Demetrio Martínez. He repaired worn and broken farm implements such as plow blades.

Pedro continued to expand and develop his landholdings. By the late 1920s, he had accumulated 1,200 acres around San José and other larger pastures near Benavides. Members of the family later heard stories that Pedro once owned land totaling 10,000 acres, but the amount of acreage at the time of partition to family members was only 3,000 or 3,500 acres. Another parcel of property belonged to Carlos Benavides, who married Juanita López, daughter of Feliciana and Pedro. Both died young, leaving a daughter named Reyes. Pedro and Feliciana adopted Reyes, but she died when she was fifteen years old. The property then passed to Pedro. Later, Feliciana also bought some land that belonged to Isidoro Benavides.

Pedro proceeded to build a new house near the intersection of the road from La Bandera and the road from San Diego to Benavides. This house had six rooms and sat at least one and a half feet above ground on a foundation of mesquite pylons, *pilones de mesquite*. People believed the height kept the rooms cooler. The house included a large living room, three bedrooms with many windows, a large porch to the south, and a

House on mesquite pylons, or piers, Duval County, c. 1908

partial porch to the west. The kitchen and dining room were at a lower level, with steps and a hall leading to those rooms. The kitchen had a large chimney to the east that still stands today. Surrounding the house were many flowering plants. Orange trees grew on the south and west, while on the north side was an orchard of fruit trees of peaches, figs, pomegranates, bananas, and some grapevines. The porch had wood ornaments, or cornices, and round wood pillars.

Pedro even had a telephone in the living room from the 1920s to the mid-1930s, plus all the modern conveniences of the day. The phone line ran to Rancho La Bandera, secured to taller than normal mesquite posts along the fence lines. Leopoldo, a son of Pedro López Jr., recalled people using the phone, gesturing with their hands and pointing directions while talking. The family made fun of these instances. Carlota, the youngest of the family, who married Mateo Valadez from La Bandera community, inherited this house. Her family lived in Pedro's last house in the early 1940s. After Pedro's death, Feliciana built a new home next to the schoolhouse. It was modern and roomy with the latest furnishings and conveniences.

In the early 1930s, Rancho San José had a large grocery store that sold fresh meat. It was owned by Pedro's son José María and his wife, Juanita. A dynamo motor, or Delco, used storage batteries and generated enough electricity to operate lights for the store and house. José María built a shaded area over the gasoline pumps so people could get gas and not get wet when it was raining. The store had a large storage room, where 100-pound sacks of beans, potatoes, sugar, and other merchandise were kept.

About 100 yards behind the store, near a gate to the pasture, was a slaughter area. A heavy crossbeam lay across two large, thick posts holding heavy tackle for raising big carcasses like cows. These carcasses were hung by the hind legs and skinned. The butcher used a large hacksaw, cutting all the bones to the spine, separating the carcass in half. Around the other side of the store was a smaller slaughter area for butchering sheep and goats.

Pedro died of typhoid fever on June 1, 1929, in Kingsville at the home of his brother-in-law, Ponciano Adame, and his wife, Crisanta Lizano. He was buried in the San José Cemetery.

Feliciana and her family continued with the ranching operation. She built some good corrals of heavy, rough lumber and added an implement shed on the south end of the corral. She used smaller cutting corrals to separate the cattle. Storage sheds housed the hay and other feed. Later, the old school was converted to a storage room. Here, in 1934, they kept wooden yokes, or *yugos*, for harnessing oxen. About 1940 Pedro López Jr. gave the *yugos* to his son-in-law Tomás Juan Benavides Sr. One *yugo* was made into a double lamp decoration and given to Raúl Tijerina, a *compadre*, or friend, of Pedro Jr. The lamp hangs at the Santa Anita ranch house near San Manuel. Raúl Tijerina and Herlinda Canales Tijerina were the first *padrinos*, godparents, at the wedding of Tomás Juan Benavides Sr. and Teresa López on Rancho San José.

In the mid-1930s, softball games were played in a cleared area on Rancho San José. The teams came from San Diego, Benavides, and nearby communities such as Concepción and La Bandera. The teams were not organized and just played for fun on weekends. Family members remember having fun because some players could not take the teasing or ribbing. When those players were at bat, they would get angry, miss the ball, and throw tantrums. Everyone laughed at the temper tantrums and had a good time.

With the drought of 1935, water sources dried up. Feliciana rented some land belonging to Mr. Billin near El Bordo. The cattle were herded to water there by Pedro Jr., his son, Leopoldo, and grandson Raúl Valadez, along with other cowboys from the area. Leopoldo remembered going with his father to check on the cattle at El Bordo. A hill called La Calawala had caves possibly used by the Indians. Inside, water dripped into a saucerlike structure, and there were a lot of rattlesnakes. The hill was made of solid rock with large cracks. Huge snakes took shelter in the deep cracks. The family members used the word *sierpes*, meaning serpents or large snakes.[26]

Another family story tells of a cousin who was taking a nap in a hammock. While he slept, a centipede, *ciempiés*, crawled on his neck and stung him. When he woke, he found the centipede stuck to his neck. He tried to pull it off but couldn't, because centipedes cling to their victim with their claws. It was finally pulled off, but the poor young man went insane. Evidently the incident affected him emotionally or mentally, for he never fully recovered his sanity. The cousin's name was omitted in the telling of the family story.[27]

---

[26] Interview with Alejo López, a grandson of Francisco López.

[27] Information is from Pedro López Jr. to his grandson Tomás Juan Benavides.

35

Curanderos and Doctors

In the late 1800s, there were few doctors in this area, perhaps because of God's Divine Providence. When sickness struck in this isolated area, the ailing person was loaded onto a buckboard, a *carretela*, or put on horseback and taken to see a faith healer. Two faith healers were Mr. Bruno in the Refugio area and Don Pedro Bazán at the La Mota Ranch. If the person was seriously ill and could not travel, a relative described the symptoms to Don Pedro Bazán, and he gave a prescription, or *receta*, to effect a cure. The *recetas* consisted mainly of herbs found wild in the pastures or herbs commonly grown in the garden. The herbs were boiled as a tea, used in baths at certain hours of the day, or taken in plain water in a specified manner. One procedure called for drinking it with the left hand, facing in a certain direction or at a specific time for three, seven, or nine days. The remedies were simple. It seems the critical ingredient was a person's faith that a patient would get well. Other people traveled to Rancho Los Olmos near Falfurrias to see Don Pedrito Jaramillo.

Don Pedro Bazán, healer

Ydolina was taken to see Don Pedrito Jaramillo when she was seven years old because of a growth in her head. It was a tumor, but at her age she could not undergo surgery. Don Pedrito prescribed the boiling of an herb and a mixture of other herbs and ingredients to make an ointment that was applied to the tumor. With the ointment, the growth of the tumor was contained. At age sixteen, Ydolina had surgery in Laredo to remove the tumor. She was too young to remember the ingredients or the herbs used to make the ointment. Don Pedro Bazán at La Mota effected other incredible cures.

In the early 1930s, a doctor named Simon García was practicing medicine in the ranches around San José. He had attended medical school, but, lacking funds to complete his studies, he dropped out before taking his degree. Dr. García, called El Profesor, lived in Lopeño, Texas, until his wife died. He came to the ranch community of San José with his three children: Simon Jr., his oldest son; Seferino, another son; and a daughter, Ester. He lived in a small house behind Encarnación Peña and Santos López's ranch between San José and El Guajillo Ranch. While living there, El Profesor befriended their daughter Santitos. Her parents at first objected to their marriage because she was young and he was in his late 40s, but El Profesor and Santitos prevailed. They married and moved into a larger house close to the side of the road. El Profesor continued treating people, gaining their confidence as many patients came to see him from the surrounding area.[28]

El Profesor got his license to practice medicine after a group of responsible citizens went to Austin as character witnesses to plead for the need of his services in the community. The witnesses included Deputy Sheriff Teodoro Sendejo from San Diego; José María López, a storeowner; and others from the community and county. He was granted a license to practice medicine.

El Profesor carried a black bag on his calls and checked the patient's vital signs as all doctors do. What was unusual at the time, however, was that the medicine he prescribed was in powder form and that he carried the medicine with him in his bag. He would pour the powder on a large piece of paper, divide the doses, and place them in small squares of paper. He folded them separately, telling the patients the time intervals that they should take each dose of the medicine.

El Profesor had his office in the front living room of his house. The patients sat and waited in chairs. On a small table, a stuffed rattlesnake with its head in a striking position sat coiled around a dried mes-

---

[28] Information provided by Teresa García Valadez of San José.

quite stump. The entire decoration was painted black. The patients went to another room in the house for consultations. El Profesor made house calls at neighboring ranches as far south as Santa Cruz, Concepción, La Bandera, and all the ranches around San Diego and Benavides to see patients too sick to visit him. His oldest son, Simon Jr., was his driver on these trips. When El Profesor returned from making house visits, patients were waiting for him. From the early 1930s to the mid-1940s, he treated patients with all kinds of diseases and delivered many babies.

El Profesor also had the gift of healing like the faith healers. He prescribed herbs and baths at different times of the day for some illnesses and also held seances at his home on certain nights. The people who attended the sessions wanted to contact a deceased relative, posing a question that only that relative could answer or asking for advice or guidance. My parents attended some sessions at El Profesor's house. One was held at our house when I was eight years old. During the sessions, the house was dark. As we played outside, we could hear the voices.

Another family story relates that once, at the school on San José, El Profesor was seen before dark dressed in a white robe. He was with two young men from the community, who also wore white robes with red crosses on the front. They helped him spread a white linen sheet across the room. People from the neighboring houses attended the rituals. Supposedly, many people talked to their dead sisters, brothers, or parents. In the rituals, El Profesor probably acted as a medium for the spirits.

During these years, when a person from the community was seriously ill, El Profesor gave the patient an antitoxin, *contra veneno*, to counteract the poison. The close relatives of the patient were told that if the sick person survived the next twenty-four, forty-eight, or seventy-two hours, then he or she was going to live. The people at the time tried herbs or home remedies learned from their ancestors for a few days, but, when they saw the patient was close to death, they called a doctor or El Profesor. By then the patient's blood was toxic, or poisoned, and the doctor used an antitoxic medicine. He evidently used it in small doses so as not to kill the patient, hoping to neutralize the poison in the system. The use of the words *contra veneno* implied an effort to stabilize the patient's condition so the medicine worked and healed the patient.

At the time, most people had relatives who had lost as many as three children between the ages of eight and fourteen. Many died of pneumonia that developed from a simple cold, while others died of an ear-ache or ear infection. Parents tried home remedies until the child died from lack of proper medical attention. El Professor moved to Houston in the mid-1940s, where he continued practicing his profession and became a member of the order of Rosicrucians.[29]

A person who knew El Profesor when he was in Lopeño, Texas, knew of the healing powers he possessed. It was claimed he could look at a person's forehead and identify what was not functioning right in the person's body. His skill was like a gift of the supernatural or occult science. One of the cures El Profesor performed was for a six-year-old girl. Reportedly, she started whining just before dark and continued until late at night. Her mother tried to make her stop, offering her anything she wanted to eat or drink, but she just kept on whining. She was spanked and sent outside, but nothing made her stop. Her mother took her to El Professor and explained the problem and what she had done to try to treat the child. He said, "Such infamy! [*Que infamia!*] You could have killed her, and she would not have stopped." He told them she had something wrong with her stomach; she had an acidic stomach, *un esteárico en el estomago*. He prescribed three baths daily, using fresh water each time, for three days. She was reportedly healed.

One time El Profesor received a letter from a woman telling of her husband's illness. She added that her husband had lost his job because of his illness, and his doctor was not helping him at all. Her letter described all the symptoms. El Profesor gave him a prescription of medicines to take. A few months later, when the patient was well and started to work again, he mailed El Profesor a gift of $1,000 as a token of thanks. El Profesor also helped another doctor who owned a clinic and practiced in San Diego in the early years.[30]

---

[29] Information provided by Santitos Peña, granddaughter of Pedro Sr. The Society of Rosicrucians is an ancient worldwide order with an interest in the occult and mystical subjects. Its aim is to provide mutual aid and encouragement in resolving the great problems of life.

[30] Information is from Hortencia García Moya now living in Livingston, Texas, whose father once lived on Rancho San José.

36

Don Eufemio, the Veterinarian

On the land that Florentino inherited near Benavides, Texas, an elderly man named Don Eufemio remained at the ranch caring for his livestock. Don Eufemio grew up on a large *hacienda* in Mexico and was a *campesino*, a man used to living on the open range, knowledgeable in the ways of nature and livestock. When the ranchers started losing cattle because of some disease, Don Eufemio was called for advice in providing a cure. For black leg disease, he would insert a garlic clove, or *diente de ajo*, in the neck, close to a vein of the cow. This would stop the epidemic. At other times, when a cow or a horse could not see, he made a small incision in the veins with a sharp, thin knife blade. This process was called a bloodletting, or a *sangría*.

Other times livestock might have difficulty walking, standing, or eating. Don Eufemio was called to cure them. In an incident in the late 1930s, Praxedis Sáenz had a horse that could not get up. It could lift only its front legs; its hind legs did not move. Don Eufemio came and effected the *sangrías*, cutting into the veins of the hind legs just above the hoofs and some additional veins higher in the legs. A day later, the horse got up and was well again. Don Eufemio may have learned this from someone in Mexico.

The ranchers of the time also used the services of an elderly *ranchero* who knew how to castrate their calves, horses, and hogs. Supposedly, this was done during the full moon, the *luna maciza*. They claimed that at this time the animals had more blood towards the head. If the animals were castrated any other time or during the new moon, they bled to death. If they somehow survived, they took a long time to heal.

37

The Children of
Pedro Lõpez

Pedro's family began to marry and strike off on their own between 1915 and 1927. The daughters married men from around the community, and most of the sons remained on Rancho San José after their
marriages. At this time, Pedro sold his sheep and goat herds to Anastacio

Wedding of Samuel López (grandson of José Antonio López) and Cleotilde Garza, c. 1927

Sáenz of Rancho El Mesquite Bonito and started buying beef cattle, which
required less care, so he would not have to hire extra help.

The family members started going their own ways. Pedro Jr. settled
in a house across the road from his father. José María built his house next

to Pedro Jr.'s house and built a store next to it. Florentino built his house next to the store. In the late 1930s, Florentino moved his house to Benavides. Eduardo also lived on San José in a house north of the school-house. María, Eduardo's wife, inherited some land on Rancho El Bordo near Bruni, and oil was struck on her land in the middle 1930s. She later built a beautiful home in Benavides with all the latest conveniences and home furnishings.

Jesús López, the adopted son of Antonio López, bought 2,500 acres of land in El Bordo at 25 cents an acre. Oil was discovered on his property also. Floyd Bennett developed this property known as the López Field. All members of Jesús' family enjoyed good royalty revenues from this property for many years.

Raúl L. Valadez was a grandson of Pedro and Feliciana. They raised him from the time he was eight months old, when his mother, Braulia, died. In 1928, when he was ten years old, he got up early to go with whoever was driving the mule-drawn wagon with cotton to the Calvin North Gin in Benavides. When he was thirteen years old, "Mamá Chana," his grandmother, bought him a saddle so he could go on the cattle drives. Family members would drive forty to sixty steers towards Freer over country roads to sell them to large ranchers in the area. It was not uncommon to drive along the country roads in the area and meet cowboys driving herds of cattle even as recently as the 1940s. There were no large trucks or trailers hauling cattle as there are today.

38

Partition of Pedro and Feliciana's Land

On October 22, 1934, the land and cattle at the ranch near Benavides were partitioned to the living male heirs of Pedro and Feliciana López, including Pedro Jr., José María, Eduardo, and Florentino. Another parcel of land on Rancho San José totaling 1,200 acres and all the livestock, property, and buildings were divided among the five daughters: Santos, Braulia, Victoria, Carlota, and Ydolina. Feliciana retained a 200-acre homestead. Pedro López Jr. was executor and administrator of the will.

Feliciana lived another eighteen years before she suffered a stroke that left her with partial paralysis. A few days later, complications set in, causing her death on May 9, 1952, about a month before she reached the age of ninety. She died at the house of her son Pedro Jr.

Raúl, a grandson raised by Pedro and Feliciana, received a son's share of the inheritance. He also received a share of his mother, Braulia's, inheritance. Raúl, being the youngest member of the family, inherited the new house Feliciana was living in at the time of her death. He later moved the house into San Diego.

39

The Catholic Church on Rancho San José

Pedro and Feliciana had an oral understanding with the family that an acre of land was to be set aside for a church on Rancho San José. Their wish was carried out when their land was divided. Their daughter Victoria López Valadez raised the money, sponsoring several projects to buy a building in Premont, which was later moved to the present site of the Catholic church on San José. Community members renovated the building and donated money for windows and pews in memory of ancestors who had lived in the community. On the church's completion in the 1980s, Bishop Thomas J. Drury from the Diocese of Corpus Christi came to bless it. The church is now a mission of the Santa Rosa de Lima Church in Benavides. Mass is celebrated regularly on Sunday afternoons at 6:00 p.m.

Five acres of the land Ydolina López Sáenz inherited was later inherited by me, her son, Andrés. I dedicated the northeast corner of the property for a recreational park and community center to serve the community and stipulated that it be named Pedro López Park, in honor of the memory of a benevolent pioneer who developed the area during hard and difficult times with much love, compassion, and encouragement to all the people he touched in his lifetime.

At this time, there are no children of Pedro and Feliciana's living. The last surviving child was my mother, Ydolina López Sáenz, who related the majority of this family history in conversations with me. Her sharing became the motivating force for me to preserve this record of our family's history. She died April 7, 1987, at the age of 91 years. May her soul rest in peace.

RANCHO
EL FRESNILLO

Standing, from left: *Josefa, Santos, and Plácida Sáenz;*
sitting, from left: *Eleuterio Sáenz; his wife, Andrea Bravo; and Brígida Sáenz*

The Founding of
Rancho El Fresnillo

Rancho El Fresnillo was founded in the early 1860s by Eleuterio Sáenz and his wife, Andrea Bravo. Eleuterio and Andrea were married in Roma, Texas, on January 29, 1862. Eleuterio's parents were José Manuel Sáenz Aldape and María de San Juan Martínez, the second of José Manuel's three wives. Eleuterio's maternal grandparents were Esteban Martínez and Francisca Arévalo. Eleuterio's wife, Andrea, was the daughter of Leonardo Bravo and Josefa Vela from China, Nuevo León, Mexico.[31]

On June 28, 1850, the annual census of Guardado de Arriba in Tamaulipas, Mexico, recorded Eleuterio as being ten years old; his brother Agapito, fourteen years old. Their father, José Manuel, was fifty-five years old, and José's third wife, María Villarreal, was twenty-five. Thus, Eleuterio must have been born in 1840.[32]

In the early 1850s, Eleuterio, Agapito, and their younger brother, Cecilio, came north to visit some relatives in South Texas. The relatives owned a ranch named Rancho Concepción, where the three boys stayed for a while, later finding work as shepherds and farm hands. Eleuterio's younger brother, Cecilio, eventually returned to Mexico. It may have been soon after their father, Manuel, died on March 18, 1855, in Mier that

---

[31] Andrea's parents were listed as deceased (*difuntos*) on her marriage certificate.

[32] Eleuterio had a half-brother, Policarpio Sáenz, whose wife was named Paula Leal. He also had a half-sister named María del Refugio, who married Antonio María Palacios from Concepción, on May 3, 1839, in Camargo, Tamaulipas. Policarpio and María del Refugio were twins, born January 25, 1823, and baptized five days later in Sabinas Hidalgo, Nuevo León. Their parents were José Manuel Sáenz Aldape and his first wife, Rita Sánchez, who were married on October 30, 1816, in Vallecillo, Nuevo León. Rita was the daughter of José Encarnación Sánchez and María Tecla Serna.

Eleuterio and Agapito decided to stay at the ranches near Concepción and Santa Cruz to make their living.

Agapito eventually married Agustina Martínez, the daughter of José María Martínez and María Julia González. The González family had purchased land from the Elizondo family and later held large tracts of land in Santa Cruz. The Martínez, Villarreal, and González families both inherited and purchased land from the descendants of Dionicio Elizondo, who was the original grantee of El Señor de la Carrera grant in Nueces County. The grant, at first called La Elizondeña, covered approximately 10,096 acres of land.

Within several years of their arrival in Texas, Eleuterio and Agapito had greatly increased their assets. In the early 1860s, the county tax assessment rolls listed each of the three brothers as paying a poll tax of 25 cents each. They owned no property at the time. By 1868, however, the tax assessment records in Nueces County, Precinct 3, listed Eleuterio as owning 100 acres valued at $50, two horses valued at $50, and 700 sheep valued at $700. Later, in 1872, the records showed that he owned 160 acres of land, and he continued to buy land. On November 26, 1883, he bought land for 175 pesos from Mrs. Virginia Fierros, according to a document from Camargo, Tamaulipas, Mexico. [33]

Eleuterio accumulated this property within six years of his marriage to Andrea. Considering the bare economy of those years, he and his wife worked hard to save money to expand their holdings in land and livestock. It was necessary to depend on other family members for help. Older people of the area say that families helped each other by providing young families with livestock and sometimes land to help them get started. The stock consisted mainly of sheep and occasionally a horse for transportation. Eleuterio probably got started this way.

His success in buying land and cattle is admirable. He was evidently unable to read and write: in the documents, tax assessment records, and warranty deeds, witnesses signed for Eleuterio because he could not write his name.

---

[33] Duval County Land Records, San Diego, Duval County, Texas, June 5, 1886.

2
The Eleuterio and Andrea Sáenz Family

Eleuterio and Andrea lived a simple and peaceful life, kept busy raising a family and working the land. The family was evidently brought up with much love, encouragement, and respect for the laws of God. They were a grateful and happy people who celebrated religious feasts and other

Eleuterio Sáenz with sons Andrés and Anacleto

festive occasions. They were brotherly and compassionate and shared in their good fortunes. Some were musicians. Most were very humble and simple people. But the hard work and the hard times took a toll on their health. Andrea eventually lost her eyesight. Eleuterio sometimes stayed for a few days with his daughters, Plácida, Josefa, and Benigna. He died June 19, 1908, at the age of 72, while staying at the home of his daughter Benigna. His wife, Andrea, died on October 13, 1917, at the age of 69, at the home of her daughter Josefa.

After Eleuterio's death, the family kept working together, perhaps under the guidance of their mother and elder members of the family. Their sons and daughters all stayed together as an extended family even after the death of Eleuterio and Andrea. The 479.7 acres that the family had held in common from Eleuterio and Andrea were legally divided on January 20, 1912. Although the sons and daughters partitioned the land into equal shares of 53.3 acres each, they remained in homesteads adjacent to each other on the lands of Rancho El Fresnillo. [34]

Amado, the youngest son, lived with his family near the main ranch house. As was the custom in the early times, the youngest member of the family inherited the house and the portion of land surrounding the family home. Amado's ranch continued to be known as Rancho El Fresnillo. Andrés, the oldest, also lived nearby with his family.

After the partition was executed in 1912, Eleuterio's and Andrea's sons and daughters gave their small ranches new names. Anastacio, for example, called his ranch "El Mesquite Bonito." Benigna named hers "San Vicente." Plácida's ranch was called "Agua Dulce," Josefa's ranch was "Santo Niño," and Andrés's new ranch was "San Andrés."

---

[34] On January 20, 1912, a partition deed was recorded in Book 6, pages 5 through 14, indicating that Eleuterio and Andrea divided their land and other properties among their family members. The Deed of Partition reads that the heirs in law held in common 479.7 acres, 239.85 acres inherited from Eleuterio Sáenz (deceased) and 239.85 purchased from Andrea B. de Sáenz, a surviving widow. All heirs inherited 53.3 acres each.

3

Papá Andrés and Mamá María

This family history now narrows to the story of Andrés and María Engracia, whom we lovingly called Papá Andrés and Mamá María.[35] In the latter part of 1912, after the partition of the land, Andrés told his wife that after harvesting the crops in the coming year, he was planning to move their house to the land that he had inherited from his parents, Eleuterio and Andrea Sáenz. Papá Andrés renamed the ranch San Andrés.

In the early part of 1913, Papá Andrés asked his brother-in-law, José Barrera, to drill a water well on the

María Engracia Villarreal and Andrés Sáenz, paternal grandparents of the author

ranch. Mr. Barrera used a pounding machine, a *máquina de golpe*, which required two mules to go around and around in a circle pulling an extended lever attached to a large gearbox. The gearbox pulled a cable that raised a heavy pipe vertically to a temporary tower at a great height and then dropped it down to the ground. The repeated pounding into the well hole made it deeper. After weeks of pounding, the well was finished and cleaned out. It produced good drinking water.

---

[35] While mamá and papá refer to one's mother and father, the terms, particularly when coupled with a first name, also refer affectionately to one's grandparents.

The night the well was finished, Papá Andrés and Mamá María hosted a festive celebration called *un festejo*. Because Papá Andrés could play the accordion, they had a dance in their house. For the *festejo*, they decorated the branches of the fruit trees around the house with oranges and apples for the children. All the relatives and neighbors came to dance, eat, and celebrate with them on this joyous occasion. These pioneering ranch families were a grateful people who enjoyed celebrating happy occasions.

Later, the water well was rigged with a mesquite-branch handle as a levering device to pump water up to ground level. Maintaining water for the family was the women's responsibility. They filled a trough for the livestock and also kept two barrels, called *barricas*, near the porch filled with water for home consumption. Natalia and Anastacia remember that, during the summer, they had to carry buckets of water for the hogs as well.

To prepare for the corn harvest that year, Papá Andrés and his sons built a corncrib, or *chapil*. The *chapil* was made of mesquite branches laid horizontally on side posts. It had a thatched roof to protect the corn from heat, sun, and rain. The men built it close to where they planned to move the main house, and that year they stored the corn crop in their new corncrib.

Unfortunately, Papá Andrés did not live to see the year's end. He passed away shortly after hosting another family celebration. It had been the family's custom to celebrate some of the feast days of the Roman Catholic saints. On June 24th, the feast of St. John the Baptist, known in South Texas as el día de San Juan, Papá Andrés took his accordion to serenade, or *dar serenatas*, his sisters and brothers at their homes.

That particular day it rained continually and was unusually cold; Papá Andrés got wet going from one house to another. He caught a cold, and the fever lasted a few days, then he contracted pneumonia. He was in a lot of pain, and finally the family decided to take him to see Dr. Strickland in Alice, Texas. Since it had been raining for many days, the creek, or *arroyo*, at La Bandera was in crest and very deep in places. The family decided Papá Andrés should stay at Felix Valadez's house while they sent someone for Dr. Strickland. The home of Felix Valadez and his wife, Leonardita, was a one-room frame house. Natalia was only five years old at the time, but she remembers her father lying uncomfortably on a mattress in a lot of pain. Anastacia was only three years old and does not remember anything about her father. The doctor arrived and gave him some medicine, but it was too late to help him. Papá Andrés died at 3:00 p.m. on July 4, 1913.

The family wrapped his body in white sheets and loaded it onto the mule-drawn wagon to take it home. Since it had been raining, they secured wooden bows and canvas over the wagon. With the ground so wet, they had to avoid the lagoons, crossing gullies and washes, or *derramaderos*, away from the regular road tracks. The rain continued all day long.

It was a very sad day for the family. They cried all the way home inside the wagon. Praxedis, who had just turned eighteen, was the oldest son. He always referred to that day as the saddest day of his life. He never celebrated the 4th of July again.

The family finally arrived at Rancho El Fresnillo late that afternoon. They placed their father's body, still covered in white sheets, on the kitchen table to lie in state. To sanctify the site, they placed crystal glasses with white candles held upright by kernels of corn. The six white candles burned all night long. They later changed his clothes and placed him in a coffin.

Papá Andrés was buried on July 5th, 1913. A mule-drawn wagon took his body to the cemetery at Santo Niño. As was the custom, the family and friends walked behind the wagon all the way to the cemetery. Papá Andrés was a member of the Woodmen of the World Insurance Society, so his tomb marker is the kind used for members of that particular association at that time.[36] After the burial, the family went into an extended period of mourning. Families mourned the death of a very close relative for one year, although younger people sometimes mourned for only six months.

---

[36] The Woodmen of the World, founded in 1890, is a fraternal organization providing various benefits, including death benefits, to members and their families. Their grave markers are characterized by various log designs.

4
Life without Papá Andrés

The sudden death of Papá Andrés left nine fatherless children, five sons and four daughters. Praxedis was the oldest, followed by Eugenio, Eleuterio, Eustorgio, and Andrés Jr. The youngest child, Andrecito, died on March 14, 1914, when he was about one-and-a-half years of age.

The Sáenz family—standing, from left: *Guadalupe, Eleuterio, Eustorgio, Andrés, and Eugenio Sáenz;* sitting, from left: *María Engracia Villarreal, Flavia, and Praxedis Sáenz, October 6, 1907*

Anastacia had a faint memory of her small, light-complexioned brother, Andrecito, crawling on the floor and under the beds. The daughters were Guadalupe, Flavia, Natalia, and Anastacia.

Another child, Florencia, was born after Flavia. Florencia died of hydrocephalus, or *marsusuelo*, a birth defect in which the cranium of the brain does not fuse together and swells with liquid, causing infection, convulsions, and death.

After Papá Andrés's death, Praxedis, at age twenty the oldest son, and Mamá María took charge of the family. They led the family with a great deal of love, respect, and obedience to the elders and raised the family members in harmony and unity. Decisions were made in everyone's best interest. They struggled along together through good times and bad.

One near disaster after the death of Papá Andrés drew the family even closer together. In the final months of 1913, the older male mem-

From left: *Flavia, Anastacia, Natalia, and Guadalupe, the four daughters of Andrés and María Engracia Villarreal Sáenz, c. 1925*

bers of the family were burning prickly pear cactus for the cattle after all the field crops had been harvested. They burned cactus every afternoon to supplement the livestock's diet of dry grass. The burning of prickly pear was done over an open fire. The men punctured the cactus paddles with a forked stick and passed them through the fire to burn off the thorns. The thornless leaves were then fed to the cattle. The thick trunk of the cactus plant was also passed through the fire and chopped into small pieces with a machete. One afternoon a strong wind came up after they had covered the fire with sand to put it out. The wind evidently uncovered the fire; it re-ignited and spread through the dry grass and burned the corncrib that Papá Andrés had built.

At the beginning of 1914, the family began to make improvements on the main house to better serve the expanding family. That year they moved the house from Rancho El Fresnillo to Andrés's property. The house was a large one-room wooden frame house with a wood floor. A separate kitchen had a large rock chimney. The house was lifted and set on wagon axles drawn by mules. The workers used several sets of axles and also several teams of mules and horses to pull the house into some road tracks alongside the edge of the field. This one-room building was placed with the front door facing east, the exact opposite from the direction that it had previously faced. Later Praxedis and his brothers built a lumber partition to divide it into two rooms.

On another trip, they hauled the kitchen. In the region, almost all of the kitchens, which had dirt floors, were built separate from the house. The family detached the kitchen from the chimney, so, because it had no floor, it was not excessively heavy to move to the new location. They again kept the old kitchen separated from the house, placing it a few feet away in a northwest direction. They then used it as a storehouse or implement shed called a *cochera*. The old chimney was left on Rancho El Fresnillo.

The family built additions to the house as the need arose. When Praxedis married, he added a new room to the north. When Eugenio married, a new room was added to the south side. Around 1925 Praxedis built his own house near Santa Cruz, and Eugenio constructed a house at Rancho La Gloria. When Eleuterio married, he moved into the room that Eugenio had vacated. The family eventually added a large porch on the east side of the house and put wooden shutters over the windows of the rooms on the west side, protecting the rooms from the sun.

5

The House Chores

After cooking and housecleaning, laundry was the most difficult chore for the women of the house. Those doing the laundry were usually Mamá María, Lupe, and Natalia. They would start early, just after breakfast, by loading the dirty clothing into the mule-drawn wagon. They took along a black iron kettle called a *paila*, a wide board, matches, and kerosene for starting a fire. Then they proceeded to one of the lagoons.

They had a choice of three or four nearby lagoons. One was close to Tío Anastacio's ranch; another was close to Agua Dulce. The lagoon of Don Merced lay the farthest away, next to Don Telésforo Garza's ranch. When the women arrived, their first step was to start a fire for the kettle and fill it with water. As the kettle began to heat, they put the clothing in to boil. Next they sliced the soap into the boiling water. They added bluing to the *paila* when washing the white garments. They laid a wide board near the water's edge for kneeling on as they scrubbed and rinsed the clothes. They stood on the board to squeeze out the soap when rinsing. Then they hung the clothing or spread it on the bushes to dry by sun and wind. At noon they ate their lunch, which included watermelons or cantaloupes when in season. After the clothing dried, the women gathered it and returned home.

Another difficult chore was grinding the kernels of corn into meal for cooking. Mamá María had a corn grinder called a *molino* to grind the cornmeal, or *nixtamal*, for the corn tortillas, and the girls had to grind a bucket of *nixtamal*. Anastacia said that whenever it was her turn to grind the *nixtamal* for the *masa*, she would throw some to the hens and chickens. When Mamá María finally caught Anastacia throwing the corn to the chickens, she commented, "No wonder when you grind the corn, the *masa* does not go far enough!"

Flour tortillas were considered a treat. They were sometimes served as a snack between breakfast and the noon meal, called *almuerzo*. The family also ate flour tortillas for an afternoon snack between lunch and supper, called *merienda*. On occasions, for *merienda*, the women baked leavened bread made with yeast, called *pan de levadura*, or cakes.

The corn had many uses. They brought the cobs from the corn-crib, or *chapil*, and used a scraper called a *desgranadora* to separate the grains of corn from the cob. The *desgranadora* was attached to a wooden box to gather the grains. The family put the grains into sacks and loaded them onto a mule-drawn wagon, which they drove to a ranch near El Saltillero that had a gristmill. There the corn was ground into cornmeal. From the cornmeal, the family made many kinds of food: cornbread; bread cookies called *panochitas*; toasted cornmeal called *pinole*; pudding, or *atole*; and other desserts. They used cornmeal as a thickening agent for meat dishes and as an ingredient in *champurrado*, a sweet drink made from cocoa, cornmeal, sugar, water, and milk. Besides using the kernels of corn, they also used the corncobs, *las mazorcas*, to feed the poultry and the hogs.

6

Working the Land

Once the family had settled on Rancho San Andrés, they dedicated themselves to the work at hand. Indeed, they produced all the basics that they needed with their own labor. On their ranch, they grew their own food, sewed their own clothes, and created their own music and entertainment. As a very self-reliant family, they subsisted on their garden products and raised cash crops and livestock for market as well. All their relatives and neighbors were also farmers.

Eleuterio, Eustorgio, and Eugenio Sáenz, c. 1908, at San Andrés

Besides working the land, the family earned money in other ways. Natalia remembers that around 1919 or 1920, some members of their family worked to help clear a road from Santa Cruz towards San Diego. Each family was given a mile of road to clear. They cleared the high area and removed the rocks from the road. Eustorgio, Natalia, and Flavia all worked for a while. About 1921 Praxedis, Eugenio, and Eleuterio worked with a land scraper pulled by mules, called a *fresno*. This family also earned money with their music. Praxedis, the oldest, even operated a barbershop on weekends for neighbors, saving them a trip into town. Later, Eustorgio learned how to cut hair and continued with the barbershop on Rancho San Andrés.

Working the land was their major occupation, however. The field crops at the time consisted of corn, cotton, beans, cane for feed, and a few rows of watermelons, cantaloupes, pumpkins, sweet potatoes, and a small row of peanuts. The family also tended a small garden close to the house, where they raised tomatoes, onions, garlic, green peppers, and cucumbers.

They did not sell any of the garden produce at market but consumed each crop as it matured. Each vegetable or fruit—watermelons; corn on the cob, or *elotes*; pumpkins, or *calavazas*; green beans, or *ejotes*; cantaloupes, or *melones*; and tomatoes and onions—had a particular planting and harvest time. The sugarcane they planted was very sweet. In the afternoons, they brought home a few small cuts of sugarcane to chew, squeezing out the sweet juice. Anastacia remembered parties where the family served cuts of sugarcane, watermelons, and cantaloupes, but all was not fun. Every member of the family had to work.

Natalia recalled working with her brothers in the field planting corn. She carried a small sack hanging from her shoulders. One of the older brothers made a row. She would count two steps and drop one grain of corn; then count two more steps, and drop two grains of corn, and follow the routine row after row. Later, corn was mechanically planted. Mules pulled a machine that had a rotating plate with holes. The holes automatically distributed the seeds at even intervals.

The corn harvest in those years was very different from today. When the corn plant matured, they would cut the head of the plant down to the first few leaves with a machete and gather it into small bundles. To tie the bundles, they used strips from yucca leaves that they made by cutting and heating the leaf until it became soft. They cut and tied the thin yucca strips together using a special knot that increasingly tightened when pulled, then gathered the bundles into a small pile, leaving them in the field for a few days to dry out. Afterwards, they used a mule-drawn wagon to pick up the bundles to move to an area where they piled them into miniature haystacks. They kept the bundles separate from the rest of the hay and fed them to the harness horses and mules used in field work.

As the workers made their next trip around the field, they cut the ears of corn from the plants and loaded them into sacks. The strongest workers carried the sacks to the mule wagon and emptied them into the wagon to be hauled to the corncrib, or *chapil*. Next, they cut the cornstalks with a machete, and someone gathered the stalks and tied them into a bundle called a *manojo*. They gathered the *manojos* and placed them into a conical circle, standing the bundles against each other where they were left to dry for a few days. The workers later hauled the bundles of cornstalks to make something like a haystack, an *arcina*. The *arcinas* were protected by log fences, or *corrales de leña*, or by barbed-wire fences so the animals did not eat the cornstalks or hay. These different kinds of dry feed were fed to the animals during the winter months.

The harvesting and planting of cotton required more work than other crops. After the cotton sprouted and grew about four inches high, the family members thinned it in a process called *desahijarlo*. They used a hoe to thin out the plants and to measure the space between them. They spaced the plants two head-widths of the hoe from one another to allow room for the cotton to grow. They left one plant one time, and then two plants, and so on row after row. Later, after the rains, the rows were cleared of weeds so the cotton could grow. Clearing the rows with the hoe was called *despaje*. All the members of the family worked in the fields doing the cleaning and thinning. Only Mamá María and Lupe, who were responsible for cooking, stayed at home.

All of the members of the family also worked during the cotton-picking season. After harvesting their own cotton, they would pick cotton at Tía Plácida's Rancho de Agua Dulce, at El Mesquite Bonito with Tío Anastacio, at Tía Benigna's Rancho San Vicente, and at Tío Amado's. All these aunts and uncles were the sisters and brothers of Papá Andrés.

In the early 1920s, Anastacia remembers picking cotton at La Gloria Ranch near Santa Cruz. Mamá María had inherited sixty-six acres of land there. No house stood on that piece of land, so they had to build a shade structure, called a *portal*, of mesquite logs. The vertical logs had a fork at the top to hold beams across the top for a roof. The family left early in the morning in a mule-drawn wagon loaded with cooking utensils and food. Mamá María came with them to cook the meals. During the day, they used the mule-drawn wagon for shade. At night the wagon provided a bed for them as well. Some of the family members slept on the pile of cotton, using the cotton sacks as pillows. Anastacia, who was the youngest of the family, enjoyed the trips to La Gloria, especially during cotton-picking season.

The family made money during the cotton-picking season. The women bought fabric with the money they earned so that Mamá María and Lupe could make the family's clothes. They also used this time as an opportunity to save their money.

The family had two mules for pulling the farm implements and their mule-drawn wagon. One was called *el macho* Dick, and the other was called *la mula* Concha. This pair of mules worked at the ranch for many years, into the early 1940s. Through the years, the mules became crafty, *maniosas*. They could unhook the corral gate with their teeth and escape into a small pasture. When Eustorgio, the youngest of the family, needed the mules, he had to search for them. They would hide motionless behind large trees. As Eustorgio moved around the bush, they would walk to the opposite side of the trees. He often had a hard time getting them to the corral to put the harness on them.

7

Feeding the Family

Natalia remembers riding to Falfurrias on a mule-drawn wagon to get salt. On the way, she and other family members visited Tía Inés, who was a sister to Mamá María. They also traveled to get bulk salt at a salt-water lake about two miles east of Falfurrias. Using a shovel, they cut small square-shaped pieces of salt and shoveled them into the wagon. After loading the salt, they visited awhile with Tía Inés and Tío Donaciano López, then returned to the ranch. When they got home with the salt, they broke it into smaller pieces and removed the dirt. Finally, they used a grinder, or *molino*, to grind it.

The salt was used for all kitchen cooking and also to preserve meat. When they had more meat than could be used within a couple of days, they cut and dried it in the sun. Besides preserving the meat, the salt also repelled flies. A few days later, after the meat dried, they put it into burlap sacks and beat it with a heavy stick to soften it. Then the meat could be folded and saved in the burlap sacks. They hung the sacks from the rafters of the house with a thin rope. To prevent rats or mice from sliding down the rope and raiding the meat, they placed circular tin plates over the sacks and tied them in place with a knot.

From a cave near the salt lake, they extracted gypsum. Many years later, a gypsum mine operated in the area. From pieces of gypsum, people made square-shaped plates and then put designs such as cupids on them. Other articles were also made that could be given as gifts.

The lard for cooking came from hog fat. The ranch family continuously was fattening one or two hogs, which they kept separate from the others. Hog pens were made of mesquite tree trunks that had been saved and stacked when the land was cleared. The logs were piled close to four feet high so the hogs could not climb out. They fed the hogs almost anything, including dried mesquite beans; pigweed, or *quelite*, a green herb abundant in the area; watermelon and cantaloupe rinds; and all the leftover food. They also fed extra corn to the hogs which they were fattening for slaughter.

When the hog was as fat as possible, the immediate family members were notified, and the entire family joined in the difficult work of the hog slaughter. Early in the morning, they started a fire under the iron kettle, or *paila*, to get the water boiling. The hog was usually killed with a hard blow to the front center of the head with the butt end of an ax. Once the hog was dead, they poured the boiling water on the hide to scrape off the hair. Afterward, they would split the carcass open to cut the different pieces of meat. The kitchen and butcher knives of different shapes and sizes had to be sharpened for various uses. Some people worked on the hog's head after removing it from the body, while others cut and cleaned other parts of the body for the various meat cuts. They set aside some meats to grind for sausage called *chorizo*. Chunks of meat were saved for frying into *chicharrones de carne*, while skin rinds were fried and became cracklings, or *chicharrones de cuero*.

Meanwhile, some family members started grinding the meat, while others cleaned the intestines, or *tripas*, to fill later to make chorizo. The meat for the sausage was flavored with vinegar and *chile colorado*.

The workers used three or four kettles, or *pailas*, for the different processes. Some people cooked the meat for the *tamales*, and others soaked the cornhusks, called *ojas*. Quite a few people worked on the *tamales*, which needed a separate *paila*. Other workers cut fatty pieces of meat to fry. When the meat chunks were good and hot, a worker dipped them out with a large strainer and put them into a burlap sack. Tying a wooden stick to each end, two workers twisted in opposite directions to squeeze out the lard, or grease, from the meat. The resulting bits of fried meat were called *chicharrones de carne*. The women saved the *chicharrones* for cooking later in various recipes. Other family members cut the skin into small pieces, fried the bits in the kettles, and again squeezed in the same manner to drain out the grease. These were cracklings, called *chicharrones de cuero*. All the grease was poured into cans to use for cooking lard.

It took all day to finish these chores. At dinnertime everyone was treated to fresh *tamales*. Each of the families who came to help received some of the food prepared during the day. *Chicharrones de carne, chicharrones de cuero, chorizo, tamales,* and a can of lard were given to each family. In this way, the work and food were shared. In a few days or weeks, someone else would kill another hog, and the community would gather to go through the same routine.

The flour used for flour tortillas was the Pioneer brand. On Sundays, when visitors came, the family served tortillas with sugar sprinkled on top and sometimes offered corn syrup with them. For everyday meals—breakfast, lunch, and supper—the family ate corn tortillas. During the pumpkin season, they made turnovers, or *empanadas,* for snacks and dessert.

The cows provided them with milk. In warm weather, the cream, called *nata,* would rise to the top. The *nata* was placed in a glass container. To make butter, a person would shake the container for a while until the butter separated in the jar. This was their butter for home consumption. The eggs the family ate for breakfast came from their hens. For special events, they might cook one of the chickens.

During cold winter nights when the moon was bright, the male members of the family hunted with their dogs for armadillos. In the cold days when there wasn't much to do, they hunted deer or javalinas. In the area around the haystacks, doves or quail came to eat the seeds. The family set out quail traps, which they made by tying wood sticks to form a

Main street of San Diego, c. 1909

box. They held the box open with a stick and attached an ear of dried corn to the stick as bait. When a bird pulled on the corn, the box collapsed, sometimes catching two or three birds.

Family members made regular trips to San Diego to buy staples for the ranch. The trip to San Diego by mule-drawn wagon took two days, one day to go and another to return. They stayed overnight with relatives in town, then returned home around dusk. At a later date, they owned a buckboard cart called a *carretela*. The *carretela* was much lighter and quicker, and they got home earlier.

The staple groceries bought in town included coffee beans, potatoes, and sugar, which were sold in 100-pound sacks. At home they stored the potatoes in a cool place to prevent spoilage. They also purchased rice, vermicelli, and soap for bathing.

To supplement the items purchased from the store, the ranch family produced their own food and sweets. In the garden and yard, they cultivated fruit trees of peaches, oranges, pomegranates, and figs, as well as prickly pear cactuses, or *nopales*, which, in season, produced tender, edible shoots called *nopalitos*. They also grew a round cactus plant that had rough thorns, called a barrel cactus, or *viznaga*. They boiled the *viznaga* with sugar and cut it into bite-size pieces, making a delicious candy. From pumpkins the family made a candy called *dulce de calavaza*. And they even made candy or jelly from beans and jelly from tomatoes and from a berry called *agarita* or algerita.

8

Home Sewing

From Mamá María Natalia and Anastacia learned early how to mend their stockings and how to make garters called *ataderas*. They learned to use the sewing machine, to crochet, which was called *tejer en gancho*, and to do many other household chores.

Guadalupe, the oldest daughter in the family, helped Mamá María with the housework. She was also the dressmaker in the family. She fashioned dresses, skirts, and blouses for the family and for neighbors who requested it. At a very early age, she started to cut materials and sew them on a sewing machine. She designed the clothes in the style of the times. The family members felt very elegant wearing the latest fashions. Lupe, as she was called, had an eye for detail in the use of buttons, laces, and trimmings. She also made clothing for the men in the family.

The children played with homemade toys. Natalia and Anastacia both played with rag dolls that had porcelain faces, hands, and feet. The rest of the dolls were of rag. Natalia's doll had black hair, and Anastacia's had blond hair. The family saved threads from hosiery to make balls for playing, wrapping a small rock with the thread until it was the size of a baseball. From the shoe tongue, called *la colilla de los zapatos*, they made a cover for the ball. They cut the leather into a peanut shape and sewed it with twine. They also played other kinds of games.

9

Ferias

Between 1915 and 1920, fairs, or *ferias*, took place during the harvest season, but, especially during the cotton harvest season of July and August, there were *ferias*. The *ferias* were similar to county fairs and were held in the communities close to their ranch. The family attended those in Benavides, San Diego, La Bandera, Filadelfia, and Concepción. In the 1930s, there were also *ferias* in the smaller communities, such as Santa Cruz, Mazatlán, and even La Tres Flores, a tiny community. The fair at Concepción was the best organized and attended and was the only one to survive into the late 1960s.

Ferias were the major entertainment in the country at the time. At these *ferias*, people visited with each other and enjoyed themselves. The people arrived in mule-drawn wagons. They placed wide boards across the wagon bed to use as seats. In later years, people traveled in their *carretelas*.

Eugenio, one of the brothers, took Lupe, Mamá María, Flavia, Natalia, and Anastacia to the *feria* at La Bandera, which was the closest to their ranch. They left about 3 p.m. and arrived at 7 p.m., when it was almost dark. On one of the trips to the La Bandera *feria*, Eugenio made a funny noise with his mouth that scared the mules. When the animals bolted in opposite directions, the wagon tongue broke, making it impossible to move any further. Eugenio fixed the wooden tongue by patching it with some fence wire, and they finally made it to the *feria*. They began the journey home around midnight, arriving about 4 a.m.

Natalia had an uncle, Francisco Ríos, whom she called Tío Pancho. He married Tía Rosa, who was a sister to Mamá María. Tío Pancho was the man who usually called out the numbers for the lottery, or bingo, called *lotería* at the Mazatlán feria. He was a very charming person with a booming voice that could be heard over the noise from the crowd.

At the *ferias* stood places to eat called *fondas*. A *fonda* was a booth enclosed with duck canvas and boards to keep out the dust and the wind. These had tables and benches inside. There were also small booths, or *puestos*, made of lumber, where vendors sold sodas; fruits; snow cones, or *raspas*; and ice cream. At the *fondas*, cooks prepared food in iron skillets over an open fire. They sold rice; beans; cowboy stew, or *carne guisada*; and country bread known as *pan de campo*. They served *tamales*; *menudo*; and goat, or *cabrito*, prepared in different ways. In addition to the food booths, other booths offered games, such as the wheel of fortune called *la manita* and a game called *los cordones*.

The visitors saw the smoke as they arrived at the *feria*, and the smell of the cooking food was everywhere. In the center of the *feria* stood a kiosk, or gazebo, called a *quiosco*, with benches for the local musicians. The *quiosco* was built at least eight feet high so the music could be heard. Benches were set on posts or pylons called *pilones* all around the town square. The ends of the long benches were left open to allow for entry from either end. Most people using the seats were mothers and small children. The young men and women walked around the square in two circles, one inner circle and one outer circle, the men circling in one direction, the women in the other. Large kerosene lamps hanging from a board nailed to the top of the mesquite posts provided light.

In some of the *puestos*, visitors could buy household articles such as dishes, vases, gift items, and articles of clothing. Many of the vendors who sold articles at the *feria* traveled around the area offering bargains in clothing, fruits, candy, blankets, and jewelry. They usually traveled in mule-drawn wagons, although later they traveled in buckboards, or *carretelas*. They also bought or traded merchandise for old objects of gold.

The names of most of these merchants are no longer remembered, except for Melecio García, whose son was named Tristan. On one occasion, Mamá María had two rings made from some gold she had, one ring for Lupe and the other one for Anastacia.

10

Entertainment

Just as ranch families provided their own food, they also created their own entertainment. The older members of the family were all musicians. They sang country songs, *canciones rancheras*, that were popular at the time. They did this for both enjoyment and practice. They were a happy family and really enjoyed these occasions.

Three members of the family played as part of a band. Members of the group were Benigno Ramón, who played the clarinet; Eleuterio, who played the saxophone and the flute; Eustorgio, who played the drums called *platinos*; Praxedis, who played the guitar and the bass, or *bajo sexto*;

The musicians—from left: Leandro Martínez, Agustine Salazar, Eleuterio Sáenz with flute, Benigno Ramón with violin, Praxedis Sáenz with guitar, and José María Martínez, c. 1924

and Victor González, who played the violin. Eugenio also could play the violin, but he played it only at home, not in public. The group played at dances, weddings, birthdays, and anniversaries. Sometimes they played serenades after the dances. The family musicians also played at the *ferias* from the 1920s to the '40s. They took part in gatherings at Premont, Benavides, San Diego, Concepción, and all the surrounding area.

The person who gave them their start as musicians was Evaristo Martínez, who had a true gift for music. From him they learned the basic chords, the tempo of music, and principles of harmony. Mr. Martínez lived close to the old school. On Friday afternoons, during the music and singing class period, he came to the school. With permission from the teacher, he worked with the students and arranged the different voices to sound like a choir.

When someone wanted to honor a relative or a friend, the musicians gave a serenade, called *dar una serenata*. It was hard to refuse a request for a *serenata*, even when a dance had ended at 1:00 a.m., because all the neighbors were related. Usually someone had a bottle of strong liquor such as tequila, which was passed around for all to drink. Praxedis said that since he did not like to drink, he would put his finger on the tip of the bottle, touch it to his mouth, and act like he had taken a swallow. These *serenatas* ended after the musicians played about three selections. By the time they arrived home, the sun was usually coming up.

When the boys started playing at events, sometime around 1915, they traveled on horseback and carried their instruments with them. Later they came in a buckboard, or *carretela*. After 1920 they used a car, arriving home about 3:00 a.m. It was difficult to get up the next day to work in the fields. It was a hard life for the musicians, but they got pleasure from seeing other people enjoy their music. This compensated them for the drain on their energy.

At first the group did not have a name, but, in the early '30s, the orchestra took a formal name. Eustorgio's wife, Rosaura, drew a picture on the side of the big drum that faced the audience. She drew a Mexican dancer called a *China poblana*, in a dance with a horseman, a *charro*. She printed the name ORQUESTA SÁENZ around the outer circle of the picture.

Another musician in the group was Benigno Ramón, their first cousin, who played the violin. Later, Benigno played the clarinet, and

Victor González from Mazatlán played the violin with the group. Once in a while, the group was lucky and persuaded Esteban Canales, father of Johnny Canales of television fame, to play with them. Esteban played the trumpet and was very charming and a lot of fun.

Esteban's father, Benito Canales, who lived at Rancho La Nacaguita near Rancho de Agua Dulce, also played the accordion. Benito was a professional musician. He played everywhere and always carried his accordion in a canvas bag. He sang the current ballads, or *corridos*, and played polkas; waltzes, or *valses*; and popular music of all types. Both Esteban and Benito were good at telling jokes.

The admission to these dances was normally 50 cents per person. The musicians were paid about ten *reales*, or about $1.25 each. It was not a money-making deal and was done mainly as fun for themselves and everyone else. The school buildings where they played were not large. People pulled the desks to the side so that mothers and girls could sit. Not much space was left for dancing. The leaders made a list of all the dancers, divided them into three or four groups, and gave them different colored ribbons so that they could take turns dancing.

The family daughters liked Saturdays because they loved to dance. They waited anxiously for Mamá María's permission to go to the dance. One or two of the brothers accompanied them. The only thing that prevented their going to a dance was when the family was in mourning. Natalia said, "Only the daughters learned how to dance." Eugenio did not like to dance, so he would make a special pumpkin candy and take it to sell at the dances. They were a happy family. They enjoyed the dances, the *ferias*, and the weddings, which lasted several days with lots of music and dancing. The dances closest to them were those at Santo Niño School. Lights for these dances came from kerosene lamps hanging inside. Once in a while, someone had a gasoline lamp, which had a small pump that forced air into the gasoline chamber and lit two asbestos mantles. The mantles burned white and gave out a brilliant light.

Yet another form of entertainment was horseracing. Anastacio kept horses at the track at Rancho El Mesquite Bonito. Another racetrack was called Veredas. On Sunday afternoons, people from the neighboring ranches would come to the races. Riding as jockey for Tío Anastacio was his son, Tomás, who also trained the horses. He was tall, slim, and light-weight. Tío Anastacio owned good thoroughbred horses that he raced all over South Texas and later in Mexico until the 1940s. Natalia remembered the family traveling to the races at Rancho El Mesquite Bonito in a Ford car around 1921 to 1924. At the races, Tía Josefa set up a canvas-covered booth, or *fonda*, where she sold plates of food.

From left: *Eleuterio Sáenz, Benigno Ramón, Praxedis and Gabriel Sáenz with Tomas Sáenz on a racehorse during the Feria de Rancho de Santa Cruz, c. 1925*

11

Travel and Transportation

Anastacia recalled traveling only to San Diego and Falfurrias. Lupe, the oldest sister, was the one who made trips into town to buy the groceries or to shop for fabric, thread, and other articles for sewing.

In the early 1920s, the family used the *carretela* to visit stores in Benavides and Premont. They were the first of the ranches to have a mule-drawn wagon, the first to have a *carretela* with two seats, the first to have a *bogue*, or a one-seat one-horse buggy. They traveled to San Diego each year to attend the masses for Papá Andrés in the one-seat buggy, which sat three people. In 1917 they bought the two-seat *carretela* for six persons. This had a roof and was pulled by two animals. It was used for hauling groceries and for family trips.

In 1918 Praxedis bought a Model T Ford for the family. This car had no glass on the sides. Instead, it had something like rubberized curtains which could be rolled up to the top of the car in good weather and rolled down when it was cold or raining. Yellow celluloid windows could be rolled down to allow the passengers to see outside. These curtains were secured to rods on the roof. The accelerator was a lever attached to the steering post. Natalia learned to drive this car. The family used it for trips or to attend mass.

On one occasion, the family made an emergency trip in the car to Guardado de Abajo, Tamaulipas, when they received notice that Eugenio was very sick. Eugenio and Eleuterio lived there in a large cabin called a *jacal*. Mamá María, Natalia, and Anastacia stayed in the *jacal* with them when they found out that Eugenio was seriously ill.

Eleuterio owned only a small herd of goats and a few hens. With no grocery stores nearby, it was very difficult to provide food for the three additional family members. They went to the neighbors and exchanged eggs for spoonsful of lard for cooking. The goats provided plenty of milk so the women could make puddings and cornbread, but they had only two small pans, and the food was not enough for all of them. Eugenio's health continued to deteriorate. His feet were swollen so badly that he could not walk. He continued to lose weight and grow weaker, so they decided to take him back to the ranch.

The family crossed the Rio Grande in a small boat about midnight. It was crowded with nine persons, and the river was at half crest. Almost at the end of the crossing, the boat got caught in a whirlpool. They were fortunate because, after a few turns, it began to move to the outer bank and made shore on the American side. As soon as they disembarked, they traveled toward Escobares to Severo Martínez's house. Their travel was difficult. Eugenio was carried sitting on a wood post with his arms on the shoulders of the front person holding the post. They had to travel very quietly to escape detection by the U.S. Border Patrol.[37] It was a long and difficult journey, but by morning they arrived at Mr. Martínez's.

Praxedis was waiting for them when they arrived, and he brought them home to the ranch. Eugenio was sick for about two years. He was so weak they fixed a special bed for him. The bed had a belt and rope with a pulley to allow them to attend him and clean and bathe him. The bed

Anacleto Sáenz

was in a room at Tío Anacleto's house across from Mamá María's. Doctor Andrés Tamez of San Diego was the attending physician. Eugenio had bedsores on his body and hips from being in bed so long. He finally got well after trying home remedies. He also had the help of a lady named Cristina Canales, who cured him of the folk disease called *ojo*. This long sickness left Eugenio in delicate health. He remained very thin physically, but he was a hard worker. He was very active, very simple in manners, and always in a joyful mood.

---

[37] The Border Patrol was created in 1924. Prior to the creation of the Border Patrol and the passage of the 1917 Immigration Act, migration across the U.S.-Mexico border was virtually unrestricted. Border residents crossed from one side to the other with little difficulty.

12

Religion

Most people living on the surrounding ranches worked hard and enjoyed life, music, and the races. Yet they were also a people with a very firm religious faith, who believed in prayer and respected God's laws. Peter Bard, known as Padre Pedro, taught the basic Catholic doctrine when he passed through the ranches. He came from San Diego, and, as he traveled, he told people when a Rosary was planned at the nearby schoolhouse or church. He taught them about the commandments and the sacraments. In the morning, he celebrated mass, ate breakfast at a neighbor's house, and then went on his way.

The church closest to El Fresnillo was on Rancho La Gloria about six miles away. The family attended church when Padre Pedro came. In the early years, most of the people came to church in their mule-drawn wagons. Father Bard died in 1920, and after that another priest visited La Gloria. The church building at La Gloria burned down about 1937.

The family learned their religious doctrine from the priest. They learned the prayers of Our Father, the Hail Mary, and the Creed and other related prayers. Their mother taught them prayers for special occasions. There were prayers for immediate danger, fear, and protection from evil. Mamá María passed on some of these prayers to them. Some of the prayers Natalia remembered are:

"Santa María del monte mayor, cuida mi casa toda alrededor."
"Holy Mary of the mount, protect my house all around."

A night prayer she said was:

"Con Dios me acuesto y con Dios me levanto."
"With God I lay down and with God I wake up."

There were prayers, or *oraciones*, for a tempest or storm and prayers to protect against poisonous animal bites when going through the pastures where the grass was high and snakes were hard to detect:

"San Jorge bendito, amarra tus animalitos con tu cordoncito bendito."
"Holy Saint George, tie your little animals with your holy cords."

In 1919, when Natalia was twelve years old, she took her first communion. All the children in the communion ceremony wore veils that their godmothers, or *madrinas*, had worn for their weddings. Shoes were made by mothers out of canvas and painted white with lime, or *cal*. The people who lived on the ranches at the time were all in the same modest economic conditions, so no one noticed the poor articles of clothing.

Natalia learned basic prayers. Padre Pedro gave small religious medals when all the prayers required for communion were learned. It was customary in South Texas for ranch families to keep religious medals and to make home altars. The little medals were taken home and hung with a piece of twine inside a niche that Papá Andrés had made with lumber and glass sides. This was a little altar where they also kept pictures and images of a favorite saint.

13

The Unforgettable
Posadas at Tía Josefa's

The following story is about the *Posadas* at a ranch in Duval County in the early 1900s. Before 1910 it was common to celebrate *Las Posadas*, a reenactment of Mary and Joseph's arrival in Bethlehem. The event has remained engraved in the minds of the children and adults of the whole community because of the manner and devotion the family attached to the ritual.

Anastacia and Natalia Sáenz in dresses made by sister Guadalupe, c. 1920

Mrs. Josefa Sáenz Barrera was an aunt to Natalia and Anastacia. She lived close to a ranch that was later named Santo Niño, and she hosted the *Posadas* in her home. Mrs. Tomasita Canales, who held these *Posadas* on a ranch named Mazatlán for many years before 1900, passed this tradition on to Tía Josefa. A woman named Doña Eulogia acted as the godmother, or *madrina*, to the Christ Child in the *Posada*.

Doña Eulogia also had a home altar with small rocks fixed in a manner and shape to represent the Holy Family of Jesus, Mary, and Joseph, as well as other saints and virgins. When Doña Eulogia died, all these rocks were placed in her coffin.

When Mrs. Tomasita Canales felt she could not carry on with the tradition of the *Posadas*, she asked Tía Josefa to continue with them. Tía Josefa accepted gladly. She received the hymns, songs, and other written materials used by Mrs. Canales. Tía Josefa learned all the hymns, songs, and other prayers by memory because she did not know how to read. Through these *Posadas*, many members of the community learned the songs, hymns, and prayers that narrated the true meaning of Christ's birth. This was carried out with a lot of love, feeling, and meaning. It helped everyone to understand the mystery of Christ's birth and to be more faithful.

The *Posadas* were celebrated at night on December 24. For many days before the 24th, all the surrounding families prepared for this event. Some nieces, including Lupe, Andreita, and Petra, helped by writing copies of all the songs, called *cantos*; hymns, called *himnos*; and prayers, called *alabanzas*, so all the people could participate.

Two brothers, Anastacio and Amado Sáenz, and their families killed a hog to make *tamales* and a pastry called *turcos*. *Turcos* were made of pie dough filled with ground pork meat, raisins, and nuts. Other neighboring families baked sweet bread called *pan dulce*, cakes and cookies, and pastries that were served with coffee or hot chocolate after the supper.

Early on the 24th, the families of all the nearby neighbors gathered to start the cooking fires for the supper. Because the nights were usually cold, they kept the fires burning outside so people could stay warm during the night. The people from the surrounding community began coming early in the afternoon. Supper was served before dark.

After supper the *Posada* began. The doors to the house were closed. One group of women stayed inside and gathered around a lantern called a *lámpara de aros*. Another group stayed outside with another lantern to sing the songs from their written lyrics. The group outside sang a *canto* asking for lodging, or *posada*, at the inn. The group inside responded in song again, refusing the room. Then the outside group proceeded with these *cantos*, moving to several of the doors and windows until they were permitted to enter. Finally, all the "pilgrims" were allowed to enter, including those representing Joseph and Mary.

Tía Josefa had two large rooms that she cleared for this ritual. She also provided benches and chairs to seat everyone. The rooms filled with women and children most of the time, while the men stayed outside. Then Tía Josefa began reciting a Rosary. At the end of each stanza of Rosary prayers, a firecracker known as a Roman candle was lit by Fabricio,

Josefa Sáenz Barrera in her home with the altar and nativity scene she made

Tía Josefa's son. These fire-crackers hurled seven balls of fire in different colors. Her brother, Anastacio, bought the firecrackers. When the Rosary ended, the people recited prayers and placed the crib and the Baby Jesus in the center of the room for the adoration.

A group of the women sang the song, or *canto*:

"Pasen a adorar al Niño,
Pasen hombres y mujeres,
Pasen todos a adorar,
que el Niño ha nacido."

"Come and adore the Child, come all you men and women,
come and adore, the Child has been born."

While the singing was going on, the Christ Child's godmothers, *madrinas*, would rock the cradle. Every man, woman, and child came forward to adore Jesus. They knelt close to the crib, kissed the Child, and gave gifts. These gifts were usually money in small denominations, such as nickels, quarters, and occasionally bills. The group also sang another psalm or hymn:

"Para remedio del hombre, nació el author de la lida."
"For the hope of mankind, the author of life has been born."[38]

There may have been other significant rituals and prayers recited at the time, but they have escaped memory since this happened more than half a century ago.

The blessing of the *compadres*, or co-parents, was another part of the Rosary. This ritual utilized a small wooden cross with flowers that hung near the altar. It required two persons who wanted to have their *compadre* relationship blessed. This might be two women or two men or one man and one woman. One person would unhook the cross and hold hands with the other person. Then the person holding the cross said:

---

[38] This is a general translation of the meaning.

"Aquí descuelgo esta cruz, en el nombre de Jesus,
pidiendo que nos de luz, y en la tierra nos consagre,
en el cielo nos veremos amadisima comadre (o amadisimo compadre)."
"Here I take down this cross in the name of Jesus, asking for
enlightenment and to be consecrated on this earth, in heaven we will see
each other, beloved *comadre* (or beloved *compadre*)."

The person receiving the cross would respond:

"Yo recibo esta cruz, con muchísima alegría, los angeles en el cielo,
y la Sagrada Virgen María."
"I receive this cross with great joy, the angels in heaven
and the sacred Virgin Mary."

After the participants spoke the words, they were *comadres* or
compadres forever. They then hung the cross for someone else to use.
This ritual is no longer practiced.

Tiá Josefa had games for the children in various rooms of the house
as well as outside. Sometimes oranges and apples were given to the children. While the adoration was taking place, sparklers were lit. The children lined up to take their turn waving the sparklers.

After the adoration, all the people wished each other a Merry
Christmas and a Happy and Prosperous New Year in a very loving atmosphere. Some of the relatives exchanged small gifts. Most of the people
brought Tía Josefa some kind of a small gift in appreciation for the *Posada*.
There was a strong atmosphere of love and unity among all the people.

After the *Posada* ceremonies, the hostess served refreshments. In
the kitchen, a large wood-burning stove warmed big pots of coffee for
everyone. After the *Posada*, the guests enjoyed sweet breads, cakes, pastries, coffee, and hot chocolate. People stayed awhile, talking until after
midnight. As everyone started home, the host family gave the departing
visitors a bag with *tamales*, pieces of cake, and sweet bread to take home.
There were midnight masses in San Diego about twenty miles away or in
Benavides about fifteen miles away as well, but at least 150 or 200 people
attended the *Posada* every year.

Tía Josefa passed away on July 18, 1958. No one remained to carry
on these traditional *Posadas*. It is unfortunate that this beautiful devotion that served as religious instruction for many people ended. In all the
years these *Posadas* were held in her home, there was never an accident,
fight, or argument among the people attending.

14

Tía Josefa, the *Curandera*

Tía Josefa was a midwife who had delivered several babies. She was also a faith healer, or *curandera*, who used herbs and prayers to heal.[39] She treated folk diseases such as the stomach illness known as *empacho*, or indigestion. Her specialty, though, was treating baby illnesses such as colic, fever, and *mollera caída*. *Mollera caída* occurred in babies not yet one year old. Signs of the illness were listlessness, fever, diarrhea, and sunken eyes that resulted from infection. It was believed that their *mollera*, or the soft spot where the cranium comes together above the forehead, had fallen in. The illness was diagnosed as *mollera caída* and cured with herbs, teas, and pastes.

Josefa Sáenz Barrera, a curandera

Tía Josefa cured other types of illnesses such as *ojo*, a folk disease sometimes called the "evil eye"; *susto*, a folk disease related to fright; and *espanto*, another folk disease related to fear. Tía Josefa also had knowledge of herbs that affected other body organs. Her knowledge had been passed on from previous generations to her. In fact, many professors in colleges, especially in South Texas, are writing now about these folk diseases and the folk remedies used by curanderas like Tía Josefa.

---

[39] For additional information about *curandera*s, see Robert T. Trotter, *Curanderismo: Mexican American Folk Healing*, 2nd ed. (Athens, Ga.: University of Georgia Press, 1997), and Eliseo Torres, *The Folk Healer: The Mexican-American Tradition of Curanderismo* (Kingsville, Tex.: Nieves Press, 1983).

Tía Josefa knew many beautiful prayers by heart, and she helped many people with her prayers, giving them comfort in times of need. Her husband, José Barrera, died in 1922, leaving her with seven children. The oldest, Santiago, was only sixteen when his father died. Although she had her share of hard times, she continued to help others.

Tía Josefa had a big heart and was a caring person of profound faith. She greeted everyone with a big hug and a warm smile. She left a legacy of love for her family, her grandchildren, and the whole community who remembered her and her kind deeds.

15

Incidents Related to the 1919 Storm

A hurricane hit the area in mid-September 1919. Tía Josefa and her family, as well as Tío Anastacio and his family, came to Anastacia's house for shelter. The wind was so strong that they braced heavy beams called *vigas* against the doors and walls. Men added their weight to the braces by leaning against them. Anastacia was nine years old and recalled two men raising her as she held a kitchen knife. They recited a special storm prayer:

> *"Jesucristo, aplaca tu ira, tu justicia y tu rigor,*
> *y con gran poder, misericordia Señor."*
> "Jesus Christ, placate your anger, your justice,
> and your severity, and with great power, have mercy, Lord."

This prayer was repeated three times. Anastacia made the sign of the cross with the knife after each recitation, symbolically cutting the cloud. After a few hours, the wind died down, and no harm came of it.

16

Education

Natalia's family stressed education and regular school attendance beginning when she was a young child. Children walked to school at Santo Niño along cow trails through fields, breaking the ice on the ground in cold weather. When the cold north wind blew, they walked close to the  trees and brush for cover. All of the family attended school at Santo Niño, including Praxedis, Eustorgio, Eleuterio, Eugenio, and all the girls in the family.

Their first teacher was Eliza Flores, an aunt to Ramón Flores from San Diego. Their second teacher was Herlinda González, who taught at Santo Niño for about six years. Two other teachers were Lupe García, who was a sister to Santana García, and the other was the wife of Jimmy Vela.

The old school at Santo Niño was torn down about 1934, when a new school was built close to the main road. It stood near Josefa Barrera's house. The teachers at the new school in Santo Niño were Margarita García, Elia Ramón, Alicia Ramón, Herlinda García, Eva González, Belinda González, Josefina Tobin, Salomé Sáenz, and Elida Wilson Alemán. Mrs. Alemán taught school three years, from 1942 to 1945. She boarded first at Diego Gónzalez's residence, the second year at Anastacio Sáenz's residence, and the last year at the Ramón residence.

Natalia

After the mid-1940s, the school building was physically moved close to the Santo Niño Catholic Church to serve as a parish center. Later, Señor Jesús Guerra bought the building and moved it to his ranch.

Natalia and Anastacia remembered how the idea for the construction of the church in Santo Niño came about. Between 1931 and 1932, the community held a big bazaar, or *jamaica*. The people held a dance and sold lots of *tamales* and plates of food. The citizens of the community also donated a sizable amount of money. The parishioners raised enough money to buy the lumber to construct the church. Tía Benigna Sáenz González donated the land. At that time, the San Diego Parish served these small mission churches. The Santo Niño church celebrated special masses and held weddings and funerals. Today no visible sign of the church remains except the cemetery a few feet to the east of where the church building once stood.

Anastacia and Natalia were the only members of our ranch family who continued their education beyond high school, attending college at Texas A&I in Kingsville. Natalia completed high school in Benavides. Later, her brother Praxedis sent her to San Diego to study under her first teacher, Eliza Flores, and another teacher, Miss Bernarda Jaime, so she could get a teaching certificate. Natalia went through a difficult period of study to get her three-year teaching certificate, as she lacked formal preparation.[40] But she tried her best to succeed at earning the certificate. She says she is forever grateful to Miss Jaime for helping her with a book on United States history. That was one of the hardest books for her.

Texas A&I College at Kingsville was founded in 1925, Natalia's first year of college.[41] She attended for two semesters, boarding at the house of Tía Manuela Arredondo. Tía Manuela was the wife of Anastacio Dávila, who lived on Lee Street in Kingsville. Natalia walked from there to college. Her professor was Mr. Momeny. Some years later, a gymnasium in Benavides was named after this professor.

Natalia taught school for one year in Santo Niño during the 1924-1925 school year. The second year she taught in a new school on Rancho San José and boarded at José María López's house. During the 1926-1927

---

[40] The 1921 certification law required that all "future" certifications would be based on college study, but a variety of levels of certification existed, with the lowest requiring only thirty hours of college work and highest requiring a bachelor's degree with twenty-four hours of education coursework including practice teaching.

[41] South Texas State Teachers College in Kingsville opened in June 1925. In 1929 the name was changed to Texas College of Arts and Industries. Then the school was called Texas A&I University at Kingsville until a few years ago. It is now Texas A&M University-Kingsville.

school year, she taught in El Guajillo. The school at El Guajillo was across from the church.

Natalia married Daniel López from the El Guajillo community on August 7, 1927, in the church at La Gloria. The wedding reception and festivities were held on San José because the church was needed for the funeral of Crisostomo Ríos, a first cousin to Natalia. Crisostomo was the son of Fabian Ríos and Natividad Villarreal, a sister to Mamá María.

Anastacia enjoyed school from childhood. She loved to play school. She and Leonor Canales helped their teacher, Herlinda García, with the smaller children. Mrs. García was so impressed with Anastacia's and Leonor's ability to teach the children songs in English and Spanish that she decided to hold a program at the end of the school year. All the older pupils prepared hard for the program, and people from the surrounding community came and applauded each song. Afterward they congratulated the students for a good performance. Everyone was happy and elated. No one wanted to go home, so a dance was held after the program. Serving as musicians were Anastacia's brothers Praxedis, Eleuterio, Eustorgio, and a cousin, Benigno Ramón. Anastacia was ten years old when this happened, so it was during the 1920 school year.

Anastacia suffered from pneumonia when she was sixteen years old. Doctor Tamez was summoned and said her condition was serious. Another doctor, Doctor González, was also consulted. No one was certain if Anastacia would get well. She believed that the two doctors and God doing the major part had saved her life. In fact, it might be said that God granted Anastacia

Praxedis and Ydolina López Sáenz, parents of the author

the opportunity to obtain a good education. In 1927 she attended Texas A&I in Kingsville for a whole year and a summer semester, boarding at Don Anastacio Dávila and Manuela Arredondo's house as her sister had done.

The first year Anastacia taught was 1928 at Rancho de Santa Cruz, where she boarded with her brother and sister-in-law, Praxedis and Ydolina. She owned her own car, so she drove to school. During all the years that Anastacia taught, she owned a light blue Ford with black fenders. The second year, she taught on Rancho Vera Cruz, boarding at the house of Victor González and his wife, Julia. The third, fourth, and fifth year, she also taught at the Vera Cruz School. This small school stood at the junction of the road leading to Rancho La Candelaria and the road leading to the ranch of Doña Francisca Vera Chapa. Over these years, she boarded with Señor Canuto Benavides; with Próspero Ríos and his wife, Gregoria Vera; at Doña Daria's ranch; at the Don Jorge González ranch; and the last year with Mr. and Mrs. Ismael Chapa. She continued attending college during the summer semesters while she was teaching.

17

The Family of Mamá María

Mamá María, who was Anastacia's and Natalia's mother, was born María Engracia Villarreal. Mamá María was the daughter of Isidro Villarreal Elizondo and Encarnación Ramón. Natalia and Anastacia had memories of their (maternal) grandfather, Papá Isidro. He had a white beard and was up in years, but he went out to the fields with his grandchildren to encourage them and give advice on working the fields. They

Isidro and Encarnación Ramón Villarreal, parents of the author's paternal grandmother, María Engracia Villarreal Sáenz

appreciated having his presence and showed him respect. He always pushed them to do more and to finish the work so there was less to do the next day.

At one time, Isidro Villarreal was the administrator of Agostadero Elizondeña. Viviana Elizondo inherited most of the land after her husband, Benito González, died, and Isidro worked for her. At a later date, Isidro worked for a few years as administrator of Saturnino Vera and Victoriana Martínez's San Buena Ventura Ranch.[42]

Isidro lived for a time in a small *sillar* house on the right-hand side of a road leading to the Vera's ranch. The house may have been on the property when Isidro bought it. The last person to live in the *sillar* home was Santiago Vera, a son of Damaso Vera and a grandson of Victoriana Martínez Vera, whom everyone called either Tía Chata or Mamá Chata. No signs remain of the house today.

By the early 1930s, only a few of the limestone blocks, or *sillares*, were still standing to mark the site of Papá Isidro's house. A hand-dug well was nearby, but there is no sign to mark the location now. The name of their ranch, Rancho La Gloria, was changed to Ríos in the late 1940s to honor a man named Cayetano Ríos, who had been a land developer in Nueces County in the 1890s.

Isidro later built a wood-frame house in the middle of this land close to the main road that passed through the ranches. The road was referred to as El Camino Real, or the Royal Road, meaning the road that the king or his government administrators traveled. Isidro built his kitchen separately, or perhaps the kitchen was used first as a *portal* and later covered with mesquite logs laid horizontally like on the *jacales*. Still later, the house was connected with boards to the kitchen, which still had a dirt floor.

Ascensión, a daughter of Isidro and Encarnación, was the youngest in the family. She was called Rosa because her cheeks were always rosy when she'd been in the heat or sun. As the youngest, she inherited the house of her parents. When Encarnación, Isidro's wife, died, he went to live with his oldest daughter, María, and her family at Rancho San Andrés. Papá Isidro was sick for a couple of weeks before he died. On the day he died, he lay down in bed. A grandfather clock stood near his bed. He told the family that at 3:00 p.m. he would pass away. That was the exact hour he died. Isidro left his land to his children. Before his death, he had ex-

---

[42] Information from Mr. Saturnino Vera, a son of Pablo Vera and Paula González, who heard it from his father.

ecuted a partition deed dated November 1, 1909. He had requested that the 394 acres that he had purchased from Nepomuceno Gutiérrez be divided among his six children, giving each 65.7 acres. The date of his death and that of Encarnación are unknown.

Following the death of their parents, Isidro and Encarnación, Mamá María's sister Sara came to live with the family. Tía Sara was always the one in charge of cooking or boiling the mixture of corn and lime, *el nixtamal*.

A story handed down in the family is that as a child Tía Sara had once fallen into a deep well and nearly drowned. Although she survived, the incident left her emotionally impaired and with a physical impairment that made it difficult for her to speak correctly. Sara was raised at Rancho La Gloria with her other sisters, and supposedly that was where she fell into the well, called a *noria de buque*.

18

The Children of Andrés and María Engracia Villarreal Sáenz

Following is a brief review of the marriages in the family. After marriage the family members continued to live at home for a few years before moving away from the family ranch to establish places of their own, where they could make a living from the land as their fathers and grandfathers had before them.

Praxedis, the first born, married Ydolina López, the daughter of Pedro López and Feliciana Adame, at Rancho San José on February 18, 1920, an Ash Wednesday. A dance was held, and lots of cakes, chocolate, and other foods were served at the wedding. Anastacia especially remembered the bean candy dessert, *dulce de frijol*. After Praxedis married, a room was added to the north side of the house. By 1925 Praxedis had built his own home on a ranch close to Santa Cruz.

Praxedis and Ydolina López Sáenz, parents of the author

Eugenio was the second in the family to marry. He married Mariana González, daughter of Manuel R. González and Francisca Ramón. The wedding was on February 11, 1921, at Rancho La Gloria in a *sillar* house that still stands. Don Carlos González and his family lived for many years in this house.[43] When Eugenio married, a room was added to the south side of the house. Sadly, today the house is in ruins and abandoned.

Eleuterio was the next to marry. He married Zulema Palacios, a daughter of José Palacios and María Salinas, on July 4, 1929, and they lived in the center room next to Eugenio's room.

Guadalupe married Hipólito Sáenz around 1936. Hipólito worked on a large farm near Petronila. The couple lived in a small house provided by the farm owner. Later they moved to a house near Praxedis's ranch. Here Hipólito farmed his own land, at the same time working as a hand on the neighboring farms and selling fruit at gatherings.

Eustorgio married Rosaura Sáenz from Guardado de Arriba, Tamaulipas. She was the daughter of Felix Sáenz and Ana María Olivarez. They married on February 18, 1933, in Guardado de Arriba and lived at Rancho San Andrés. Eustorgio was the youngest son in the family. By that time, all the other married members of the family had left to live on their own, so he took over all the work that had to be done on the ranch, such as the planting and harvesting of crops. Eustorgio also performed one of the most important tasks—the hauling of drinking water from Tía Plácida's Rancho de Agua Dulce. The first well drilled at Rancho San Andrés became salty around 1919. It seems that the well-lining tube was ruptured, and salt water seeped through. Only the horses and cattle could drink the water. Eustorgio hitched a pair of mules to the wagon carrying the three wooden barrels, or *barricas*. The team drew close to the water cistern at Agua Dulce. With a bucket, Eustorgio filled all three barrels and covered them with a heavy duck canvas tied to the top. This kept the barrels from spilling too much water on the trip. Sometimes Eustorgio was lucky, and all he had to do was move close to an overflow pipe and

---

[43] The Nueces County tax rolls indicate that in 1861 Isidro's father, Cayetano Villarreal, owned 6,640 acres of Dionicio Elizondo's El Señor de la Carrera Grant. Cayetano Villarreal married Eufemia Elizondo, a daughter of Dionicio Elizondo. The dates of death of Isidro or his wife, Encarnación, are not reflected in the church records of St. Francis de Paula Catholic Church in San Diego, which was the parish church for all these missions.

move the wagon a little closer each time to fill the next barrel. These barrels remained on the wagon at all times.

Anastacia, the youngest daughter, married Abelino Sáenz, who was from Guardado de Arriba. He was a brother of Rosaura. They married at the church in Santo Niño on May 9, 1937. The wedding ceremony took place at this ranch, and, like all the weddings of that time period, it lasted three days. They slaughtered a large cow, then barbecued the meat in a hole covered with tin and a fire built over it, to make a pit barbecue, or *barbacoa de pozo*. They slaughtered fourteen goats, or *cabritos*, and cooked the meat in the iron kettles, or *pailas*. Many neighbors came to help to make the *tortillas*, placing them in washtubs, called *baños de tortillas*, to feed all the people. There was the traditional afternoon snack, or *merienda*, with *pan de polvo*, which are the modern-day wedding cookies, and a cup of hot chocolate. At night came the dance with the Sáenz orchestra playing. The visitors slept in their cars Saturday night to be there for the wedding the next day.

Anastacia was the last to marry, leaving Mamá María and Flavia alone. Anastacia said Flavia lamented, "Now we are alone, Mamá María *y yo*, and there is no one to drive us anymore to visit or go for rides."

In the early 1930s, Eleuterio and Eugenio each had their own houses. Eugenio's was located in Rancho La Gloria across from Tía Rosa's house. Eustorgio bought a house from Rancho San Vicente about 1943 and moved it to the center west end of the field at Rancho San Andrés. There he drilled a well that provided good drinking water. Mamá María then moved her home close to Eustorgio's and lived there a few years. In the early 1950s, Eustorgio moved his house from Rancho San Andrés to a piece of land across the road from Praxedis's house. He lived there about three years and then moved his house to Alice.

After Eustorgio moved, Mamá María and Flavia were left alone at Rancho San Andrés once more. They decided to move their house close to Praxedis's house as Eustorgio had done. Mamá María and Flavia lived here for about ten years. Flavia was the only child in the family who did not marry but stayed home with her mother. She was a very good cook, an excellent housekeeper, and a very tidy person, and she acted as hostess when members of the family visited her and Mamá María. They took care of each other and missed each other when one went to visit or stay with relatives for a few days.

Mamá María died on July 20, 1961, leaving Flavia alone. A couple of years later, Flavia's house was moved to San Diego, so she could be close to her sister Natalia and medical help in case of sickness.

Here the stories of Rancho San Jose and Ranch El Fresnillo end. The history of my mother and father's families is one of families living a pastoral life of beauty and surviving the obstacles of life with love, caring, and unity. They left an example of family life and values that will be hard for future generations to emulate.

Funeral of Evangeline López, young daughter of Natalia Sáenz and Daniel López, 1930, at Santo Niño Cemetery near Rancho El Fresnillo.

Appendices

*Editor Andrés Tijerina, Natalia Sáenz López, and author Andrés Sáenz
on the Exhibit Floor of the Institute of Texan Cultures in 1998—behind them is the jacal
which was constructed from the descriptions given in Mr. Sáenz's manuscript.*

Who's Who in the Maternal Family: San José

José Antonio López

Founder of Rancho San José; baptized June 14, 1830; married María de los Santos González August 17, 1853; father of seven children; died December 24, 1903; maternal great-grandfather of author Andrés Sáenz.

María de los Santos González

Wife of Antonio; founder of Rancho San José; baptized June 17, 1832; mother of seven children; died 1878-1884; maternal great-grandmother of author Andrés Sáenz.

José Miguel López

Father of Antonio; maternal great-great-grandfather of author Andrés Sáenz.

María Marina Sánchez y Fuentes

Wife of José Miguel López; mother of Antonio; maternal great-great-grandmother of author Andrés Sáenz.

Francisco López

Oldest natural son of María and Antonio; brother of Pedro; married Petra Vela García in 1875; maternal great-uncle of author Andrés Sáenz.

Chico Reyna

Cousin of Antonio living in Mexico.

Margarito López

Son of María and Antonio; younger brother of Francisco and Pedro; married Juana García May 23, 1888.

Rodolfo López

Grandson of Margarito; great-grandson of Antonio.

Rosendo López

Son of Petra and Francisco López; married Lucia and had son, Alejo López.

Pedro López Sr.

Son of María and Antonio born October 21, 1860; married Feliciana Adame
August 31, 1878; father of 12 children including Ydolina, mother
of author Andrés Sáenz; died June 1, 1929; maternal grandfather of author
Andrés Sáenz.

Eduardo López

Son of Feliciana and Pedro born February 10, 1898; married María Lopez.

Ponciano Adame

Feliciana's brother; brother-in-law of Pedro; married Crisanta Lizano.

Gregoria López

Daughter of María and Antonio; married May 6, 1881, to Dionicio Sáenz.

María López

Daughter of María and Antonio; married April 15, 1895, to Eusebio García.

Josefina García

Daughter of María and Eusebio García; married Juan Sandoval.

José Moreno

Foster son of Antonio and Dominga Peña, Antonio's second wife.

Jesús López

Adopted son of María and Antonio; married Gavina García in 1873.

Fermán López

Son of María and Antonio; brother of Pedro; married December 15, 1880, to
Adelaida Gutiérrez.

Juanita López Adame

Wife of Reyes Adame; mother of Feliciana Adame; mother-in-law of Pedro.

Dominga Peña

Second wife of Antonio López; married December 8, 1886; died May 18, 1922.

Cleofas and Victoriana López

Close neighbors of Antonio and Dominga at Rancho San José.

José Manuel López

Son of María and José Miguel López; brother of Antonio; married María Teresa
García December 9, 1868.

María Magdalena López

Daughter of María and José Miguel López born July 25, 1849; sister of Antonio.

María Casimira López

Daughter of María and José Miguel López; sister of Antonio.

Reynaldo López

Great-grandson of Antonio; grandson of Margarito.

Mauricio López

Son of Jesús López (adopted son of María and Antonio).

Samuel López

Son of Mauricio López; grandson of María and Antonio.

Gumecinda López

Daughter of Francisco López; granddaughter of María and Antonio.

Alejo López

Son of Lucia and Rosendo López; great-grandson of María and Antonio.

Camilo Palacios

Neighbor of Antonio who later lived at Rancho La Bandera.

Ydolina López Sáenz

Daughter of Feliciana and Pedro born December 2, 1895; married Praxedis Sáenz February 18, 1920; died April 7, 1987; mother of author Andrés Sáenz.

Reyes Adame

Father of Feliciana Adame born Jan. 6, 1825; father-in-law of Pedro; died March 6, 1911; maternal grandfather of Ydolina López Sáenz.

Raul L. Valadez

Son of Braulia López and Daniel Valadez; Feliciana and Pedro raised him after their daughter Braulia's death; inherited Feliciana's new house in 1952.

José Antonio González

Owner of the La Huerta Land Grant.

José Maldonado (Josesito) and Doña Chavela

Lived in Dominga and Antonio's house in the 1930s.

Tomás Juan Benavides Jr.

Son of Teresa López and Tomás Juan Benavides Sr; great-grandson of Feliciana and Pedro.

Antonio Hinojosa Pérez

Oldest son of Luciano Hinojosa and Apolonia Pérez; came to South Texas in 1850 when 15 years old; founded the Hinojosa Ranch.

Dionicio Elizondo

Owner of the El Señor de la Carrera Land Grant in 1835.

Rufino Vela

Had property near Margarito López.

Florentino López

Son of Feliciana and Pedro born February 8, 1900; married Petra Garcia.

Santos López

Oldest daughter of Feliciana and Pedro born August 13, 1879; married Encarnación Peña.

Juanita López

Second of twelve children of Feliciana and Pedro born May 16, 1881; married Carlos Benavides.

Braulia López

Third of twelve children of Feliciana and Pedro born May 23, 1883; married Daniel Valadez.

Victoria López

Fourth of twelve children of Feliciana and Pedro born March 6, 1885; married Silverio Valadez.

Pedro López Jr.

Son of Feliciana and Pedro; married Jesusa Valadez.

Natalia Sáenz López

Daughter of María Engracia Villarreal and Andrés Sáenz born 1908; sister of Praxedis; married Daniel López August 27, 1927; aunt of author Andrés Sáenz.

Carlos Benavides

Married Juanita López (daughter of Feliciana and Pedro).

Reyes López

Daughter of Juanita and Carlos Benavides; was adopted by grandparents Feliciana and Pedro when parents died.

Leopoldo López

Son of Jesusa and Pedro Jr.; grandson of Pedro López Sr.

Carlota López

Daughter of Feliciana and Pedro; married Mateo Valadez; lived in Feliciana and Pedro's last house in the 1940s.

José María López

Seventh of twelve children of Feliciana and Pedro born July 4, 1893; married Juanita Oliveira.

José Manuel López

Son of José Miguel López; brother of Antonio.

Feliciana Adame

Daughter of Juanita and Reyes Adame born July 9, 1863; married Pedro López August 31, 1878; mother of twelve children; known as Mamá Chana by grandchildren; died May 9, 1952.

Andrés Sáenz

Son of Ydolina López and Praxedis Sáenz born Aug. 9, 1927; married Jovita Treviño; Pedro López is maternal grandfather; Antonio López is maternal greatgrandfather; José Miguel López is maternal great-great-grandfather.

Natalia Sáenz

Daughter of María Engracia Villarreal and Andrés Sáenz born 1908; sister of Praxedis; married Daniel López August 27, 1927; aunt of author Andrés Sáenz.

Anastacia Sáenz

Daughter of María Engracia Villarreal and Andrés Sáenz born 1910; sister of Praxedis; married Abelino Sáenz May 9, 1937; aunt of author Andrés Sáenz.

Andrés Sáenz, "Papá Andrés"

Son of Andrea Bravo and Eleuterio Sáenz born September 19, 1868; father of Praxedis; married María Engracia Villarreal February 28, 1891; died July 4, 1913; grandfather of author Andrés Sáenz.

María Engracia Villarreal, "Mamá María"

Oldest daughter of Isidro Villarreal Elizondo and Encarnación Ramón born April 16, 1871; married Andrés Sáenz February 28, 1891; mother of Praxedis; died July 20, 1961; grandmother of author Andrés Sáenz.

Who's Who in the Paternal Family: El Fresnillo

Zulema Palacios

Married Praxedis's brother Eleuterio Sáenz.

Rosaura Sáenz

Married Praxedis's brother Eustorgio Sáenz February 18, 1933.

Eleuterio Sáenz

Grandfather of Praxedis, Natalia, and Anastacia; born c. 1840; married Andrea Bravo January 29, 1862; died June 19, 1908; paternal great-grandfather of author Andrés Sáenz.

Andrea Bravo

Born 1846; married Eleuterio Sáenz January 29, 1862; daughter of Leonardo Bravo and Josefa Vela; died October 13, 1917; paternal great-grandmother of author Andrés Sáenz.

José Manuel Sáenz Aldape

Father of Eleuterio Sáenz born c. 1795; married Rita Sánchez October 30, 1816; second marriage to María de San Juan Martínez; third marriage to María Villarreal; died March 18, 1855; father of Eleuterio; paternal great-great-grandfather of author Andrés Sáenz.

María de San Juan Martínez

Second wife of José Manuel Sáenz Aldape; daughter of Esteban Martínez and Francisca Arévalo; mother of Eleuterio Sáenz; paternal great-great-grandmother of author Andrés Sáenz.

Esteban Martínez

Father of María de San Juan Martínez; grandfather of Eleuterio Sáenz; married Francisca Arévalo; paternal great-great-great grandfather of author Andrés Sáenz.

Francisca Arévalo

Married Esteban Martínez; grandmother of Eleuterio Sáenz; paternal great-great-great grandmother of author Andrés Sáenz.

Leonardo Bravo

Father of Andrea Bravo; married Josefa Vela.

Josefa Vela

Mother of Andrea Bravo; married Leonardo Bravo.

Agapito Sáenz

Older brother of Eleuterio born c. 1836; married Agustina Martínez.

María Villarreal

Third wife of José Manuel Sáenz Aldape.

Cecilio Sáenz

Younger brother of Eleuterio and Agapito.

Policarpio Sáenz

Son of José Manuel Sáenz Aldape and first wife, Rita Sánchez; born in 1823; half-brother of Eleuterio; twin brother of María del Refugio; married Paula Leal.

Paula Leal

Married Policarpio Sáenz.

María del Refugio Sáenz

Daughter of José Manuel Sáenz Aldape and his first wife, Rita Sánchez; born in 1823; twin of Policarpio Sáenz; half-sister of Eleuterio.

Antonio María Palacios

Married María del Refugio May 3, 1839.

Rita Sánchez

First wife of José Manuel Sáenz Aldape; married October 30, 1816.

José Encarnación Sánchez

Father of Rita Sánchez, first wife of José Manuel Sáenz Aldape; married María Tecla Serna.

Agustina Martínez

Married Agapito Sáenz, older brother of Eleuterio; daughter of José María Martínez and María Julia González.

Victor González

Played violin with the Sáenz family.

Benigno Sáenz

Son of Eleuterio and Andrea Bravo; brother of Andrés Sáenz; married Brígida Vera; great-uncle of author Andrés Sáenz.

Plácida Sáenz

Daughter of Eleuterio Sáenz and Andrea Bravo; first husband, Zacarías Hinojosa; second husband, Leandro Martínez.

Josefa Sáenz

Daughter of Eleuterio Sáenz and Andrea Bravo born March 1879; married José Barrera; died July 18, 1958.

Benigna Sáenz

Daughter of Eleuterio Sáenz and Andrea Bravo; married Vicente González.

Amado Sáenz

Youngest son of Eleuterio Sáenz and Andrea Bravo born September 1882; married Juanita Valadez.

Anastacio Sáenz

Son of Eleuterio and Andrea Sáenz born March 1877; brother of Andrés Sáenz; married Petra Valadez; uncle of author Andrés Sáenz.

Felix and Leonardita Valadez

Friends of "Papá Andrés" and "Mamá María."

Praxedis Sáenz

Oldest son of Andrés Sáenz and María Engracia Villarreal born July 21, 1892; married Ydolina López February 18, 1920; father of author Andrés Sáenz; died February 10, 1976.

Eugenio Sáenz

Son of Andrés Sáenz and María Engracia Villarreal born November 1893; married Mariana González February 11, 1921; uncle of author Andrés Sáenz.

Eleuterio Sáenz

Son of Andrés Sáenz and María Engracia Villarreal born September 1895; married Zulema Palacios July 4, 1929; uncle of author Andrés Sáenz.

Eustorgio Sáenz

Son of Andrés Sáenz and María Engracia Villarreal; married Rosaura Sáenz February 18, 1933; uncle of author Andrés Sáenz.

Andrés Sáenz Jr., "Andrecito"

Youngest son of Andrés Sáenz and María Engracia Villarreal born 1912; died March 14, 1914.

Guadalupe Sáenz

Daughter of Andrés Sáenz and María Engracia Villarreal born October 1897; married Hipólito Sáenz in 1936.

Flavia Sáenz

Daughter of Andrés Sáenz and María Engracia Villarreal.

Florencia Sáenz

Daughter of Andrés Sáenz and María Engracia Villarreal.

Tomás Sáenz

Son of Anastacio Sáenz and Petra Valadez.

Anacleto Sáenz

Son of Eleuterio and Andrea Bravo; brother of Andrés Sáenz Sr.; married María Palacios Benavides.

José Barrera

Married Josefa Sáenz; brother-in-law of Andrés Sáenz Sr.; died 1922.

Ydolina López

Daughter of Feliciana and Pedro López Sr. born December 2, 1895; married Praxedis Sáenz February 18, 1920; died April 7, 1987; mother of author Andrés Sáenz.

Isidro Villarreal Elizondo

Born May 1840, married Encarnación Ramón; father of María Engracia Villarreal; great-grandfather of author Andrés Sáenz.

Ascensión Villarreal

Daughter of Encarnación Ramón and Isidro Villarreal Elizondo; sister of María Engracia Villarreal.

Encarnación Ramón

Born 1848; married Isidro Villarreal Elizondo; mother of María Engracia Villarreal, "Mamá María"; great-grandmother of author Andrés Sáenz.

Bibliography

by Andrés Tijerina

In editing this family history of Don Andrés Sáenz, it was necessary to consult a variety of books on the history of North Mexico, the history of agriculture in South Texas, architectural styles of the borderlands, and the flora and fauna peculiar to this ranching frontier. It is tempting to expand the list of entries to cover every detail and aspect mentioned in the book, but prudence dictates that the reader would most appreciate those books and entries that would lay a firm literary foundation for this specific story. Thus, the following bibliography is a selected list of sources that compose a very concise compendium of the general literature on South Texas ranches that were part of the same frontier as Ranchos San José and El Fresnillo.

Bailey, Ben P., Jr. *Border Lands Sketchbook.* Tr. Channing Horner and Louise Bailey Horner. Waco: Texian Press, 1976.

Boyd, Douglas K., Andrés Tijerina, Karl W. Kibler, Amy C. Earl, and Martha Doty Freeman. "Pharr-Reynosa International Bridge: Continued Archeological and Historical Research at El Capote Ranch Community, Hidalgo County, Texas." Reports of Investigation No. 97. Austin: Texas Antiquities Committee, 1994.

Casstevens, Mary Anna. "The Institution of the Spanish-Mexican Ranch and Its Culture in South Texas." Unpublished M.A. thesis, Texas A&M University-Kingsville, 1997.

De León, Arnoldo. *The Tejano Community, 1836-1900.* Albuquerque: University of New Mexico Press, 1982.

De León, Arnoldo, and Kenneth L. Stewart. *Tejanos and the Numbers Game: A Socio-Historical Interpretation from the Federal Censuses, 1850-1900.* Albuquerque: University of New Mexico Press, 1989.

George, Eugene. *The Historic Architecture of Texas: The Falcón Reservoir.* Austin: Texas Historical Commission, 1975.

González, Arturo. *Historia de Tamaulipas*. 2d ed. Cd. Victoria: Libreria El Lapiz Rojo, 1931.

González, Jovita, and Eve Raleigh. *Caballero: A Historical Novel*. Ed. José E. Limón and María Cotera. College Station: Texas A&M University Press, 1996.

González, Jovita. "Social Life in Cameron, Starr, and Zapata Counties." Unpublished M.A. thesis, University of Texas at Austin, 1930.

Graham, Joe S. *El Rancho in South Texas: Continuity and Change from 1750*. Denton: University of North Texas Press, 1994.

Graham, Joe S., ed. *Hecho en Tejas: Texas-Mexican Folk Arts and Crafts*. Denton: University of North Texas Press, 1991.

Guerra, Fermina. "Mexican and Spanish Folklore and Incidents in Southwest Texas." Unpublished M.A. thesis, University of Texas, 1941.

Hinojosa, Alicia. *The Hinojosa Family: From Mier, Tamaulipas, Mexico to Texas*. Somerville: A. Hinojosa Perone, 1992.

Hudson, Wilson M. *The Healer of Los Olmos and Other Mexican Lore*. Dallas: Southern Methodist University Press, 1951.

Lehmann, V.W. *Forgotten Legions; Sheep in the Rio Grande Plain of Texas*. El Paso: Texas Western Press, 1969.

Los Caminos del Río Heritage Project. *A Shared Experience: The History, Architecture and Historic Designations of the Lower Rio Grande Heritage Corridor*. Austin: Texas Historical Commission, 1994.

Lott, Virgil N., and Mercurio Martínez. *The Kingdom of Zapata*. San Antonio: The Naylor Company, 1953.

McAllen, Margaret. *The Heritage Sampler: Selections from the Rich and Colorful History of the Rio Grande Valley*. Edinburg: New Santander Press, 1991.

Martínez, Covian, and Vidal Efren. *Compendio de historia de Tamaulipas*. XX. Cd. Victoria: Ediciones Siglo, 1973.

Montejano, David. *Anglos and Mexicans in the Making of Texas, 1836-1986*. Austin: University of Texas Press, 1987.

Montejano, David. *Race, Labor Repression, and Capitalist Agriculture: Notes from South Texas, 1920-1930*. Berkeley: University of California, Institute for the Study of Social Change, 1977.

Peña, Manuel H. *The Texas-Mexican Conjunto: History of a Working-Class Music*. Austin: University of Texas Press, 1985.

Ramirez, Emilia Schunior. *Ranch Life in Hidalgo County after 1850*. Edinburg: New Santander Press, 1971.

Texas General Land Office. *Abstract of All Original Texas Land Titles Comprising Grants and Locations to August 31, 1941*. 8 vols. Austin: The State of Texas, 1942.

Tijerina, Andrés. *Tejanos and Texas under the Mexican Flag, 1821-1836*. College Station: Texas A&M University Press, 1994.

Tijerina, Andrés. *Tejano Empire: Life on the South Texas Ranchos*. College Station: Texas A&M University Press, 1998.

U.S. Government. *The Seventh Census of the United States: 1850*. Texas mss. (microfilm).

U.S. Governement. *The Tenth Census of the United States: 1880*. Texas mss.

Valley By-Liners. *Gift of the Rio: Story of Texas' Tropical Borderland*. Mission: Border Kingdom Press, 1975.

Valley By-Liners. *Rio Grande Roundup: Story of Texas Tropical Borderland*. Mission: Border Kingdom Press, 1980.

Villarreal, Roberto M. "The Mexican-American Vaqueros of the Kenedy Ranch: A Social History." Unpublished M.A. thesis, Texas A&I University, 1972.

Xavier, Sister Mary. *Father Jaillet: Saddlebag Priest of the Nueces*. Corpus Christi: Diocese of Corpus Christi, 1948.

Zapata County Historical Society, Folklore Committee. "Zapata County Folklore." Unpublished booklet in Zapata County Museum, 1983.

Photo Credits

Page 5   Sid Williams, Pearsall.

Page 14   John Wildenthal Family, Cotulla

Pages 31, 32, 52, 54, 68, 70 William K. Hoffman Collection. Gift of Glen and Rosemary Hoffman Skaggs, San Antonio.

Page 56   Dorothy Peeler Rugh, Christine.

Page 73   O.B. Garcia, Corpus Christi.

Page 103   Ray J. Garcia, Corpus Christi

Glossary

agave	plant from which a fermented drink and candy is made; locally called maguey
agarita	algerita or barberry in English, used to dye cloth yellow, berries used to make a tart jelly
albacar	sweet basil
albañil	mason or bricklayer
alabanza	hymn of praise
almuerzo	mid-morning snack
ánimo	encouragement, courage, spirit
arcina	haystack
arroba de manteca gringa	can of lard
arroyo	stream bed
azadón de ojo	heavy-handled hoe
atadera	garter
atole	thickened drink made with cornmeal and chocolate
bajo sexto	bass
baños de tortillas	tubs filled with tortillas
barbacoa de pozo	pit barbecue
barrica	wooden barrel
bogue	horse-drawn buggy
bordo de tierra	ridge of dirt
burra	donkey
cabrito	goat
cajeta	caramel
cal	lime
calabaza	squash
caldillo	soup
caliche	soil with flakes of lime
calzoncillos largos	long johns
campesino	peasant knowledgeable about living in the open range
canción ranchera	country song
canoa	water trough
canto	song

147

carbunclo	carbuncle, malign tumor or pustule with a hard black center
cariño	love or affection
carne guisada	cowboy stew
carne seca	dried jerky meat
carretela	wagon or buckboard
carrillo	pulley
casa de piedra	stone house
casa de sillares	house of limestone blocks
casilla	voting place
cazo	kettle
champurrado	a drink made of cocoa, cornmeal, sugar, water, and milk
chancaquilla	edible root of the barrel cactus (viznaga)
chaparro prieto	kind of oak tree used to dye cloth a dark purple
chapil	corncrib
charro	Mexican horseman whose traditional outfit is highly decorated with silver
chicharrón de carne	bite-sized pieces of fried meat and fat
chicharrón de cuero	crackling
chicle	gum
China poblana	regional dress from Puebla, Mexico, which includes a full, sequined skirt and colorful embroidered top
chorizo	spicy pork sausage
ciempiés	centipede
cochera	tool shed
colilla de los zapatos	the tongue of a shoe
coma	tree whose berries produce a gumlike substance
comal	large griddle plate used to cook tortillas
compadre	friend
consejo	advice
contra veneno	antidote used to neutralize poison
corral de leña	mesquite log corral
corrido	ballad
cortar	to cut
cubo	bucket
curandera	traditional healer who uses prayer and herbs
dar serenata	to give a serenade
derramadero	spillway
desahije	thinning out a crop with hoes
desenraiz	a process used to clear land
desgranadora de maíz	corn sheller

despaje	weeding between plants
diente de ajo	clove of garlic
día de San Juan	June 24, celebrated as the day of St. John the Baptist
doctrina	doctrine
don, doña	title of respect (masculine, feminine)
dulce de calavaza	pumpkin candy
dulce de frijol	bean candy
ejotes	green beans
elotes	fresh corn on the cob
empacho	stomachache, indigestion
espanto	"fright," a folk disease
esteárico en el estómago	acid in the stomach
estafiate	wormseed, an herb used for colic
estero	estuary, body of water fed by a river
felpa	flannel
feria	county fair
festejo	a celebration or a feast
fideo	vermicelli noodles
fonda	food booth at a fair
fresnillo	ash tree, land scraper
ganado menor	minor livestock: sheep, goats, and pigs
ganado mayor	major livestock: cattle and horses
garrocha	decorated stick used to prod oxen
gato tigerio	bobcat
gente	people
granado	pomegranate tree
grano carbunco	sore with a hard black center
guajín	mule-drawn wagon
hacendado	large landowner
hacha	ax
hermano y hermana	brother and sister
himnos	hymns
infamia	disgrace
jabón del borrego	soap similar to crystal white soap
jacal	hut or shack
jacal de leña	hut built of locally available materials such as mesquite branches; often with thatched roof
jamaica	church bazaar
la manita	a game played at county fairs
la raya	finishline
la voz del cielo	voice from heaven
lama	yellow foam on water surface

lámpara de aros	lantern
las Posadas	a religious celebration reenacting Mary and Joseph's arrival in Bethlehem
los cordones	a game played at county fairs
lotería	bingo
luna maciza	full moon
macho	male mule
madreselva	honeysuckle
majada	natural corral made of cactus, mesquite logs
mandamiento	commandment
manioso	crafty
manojo	bundle of cornstalks
manteca o cebo	tallow
máquina de golpe	a drilling machine which uses a pounding motion to drill a well
marsusuelo	hydrocephalus, a birth defect in which the cranium does not fuse, causing swelling of the brain
masa	dough
mazorca de maíz	corncob
melón	cantaloupe
merienda	mid-afternoon snack
mesclía	denim
moca	tin cup
molino	hand grinding-mill
mollera caída	an illness in which the soft spot of a baby's head is said to sink in, causing listlessness and even death
mona	standing bundle of cornstalks
mula	mule
nata	cream
nixtamal	corn which has been softened by soaking in lime
nopaleras	cactus patch
nopalitos	prickly pear cactus
noria de buque	water well with bucket
ojas	cornhusks
ojo	a folk disease sometimes called the "evil eye"
olla	black cast iron pot used for cooking
oraciones	prayers
padrino	sponsor
padrino de bautizmo	baptismal sponsor or godfather
paila	black kettle or frying pan
pala	shovel
pan de maíz	cornbread
pan de campo	a bread made outdoors of either flour or cornmeal

pan de polvo	leavened bread
pan dulce	pastry, sweet breads
pan flojo	similar to pan de campo (see previous page)
panochita	cookie made of cornmeal, sugar, lard, and cinnamon tea
parrilla	grill used to cook meat
penca	prickly leaf of the maguey plant
peón	farm laborer
picadillo	ground meat or hash
pinole	toasted cornmeal
pilón de mesquite	mesquite pylon on which a house is built
pita	South Texas yucca
pitahaya	red berry from the viznaga plant
plática	conversation
platinos	literally platinum, also means drums
plaza	market or town square
portal	structure which provides shade, rain protection
presa	earthen dam
puesto	booth at a fair
pulque	fermented liquid made from cooked maguey
quelite	wild plant used to feed hogs
raspa	snow cone
rastrojo	dried cornstalk
real	monetary bit worth 12.5 cents in 1910
receta	prescription
respeto	respect
romero	rosemary
ruda	rue; bitter leaves used in medicine
sacramento	sacrament
salvia	sage; plant used to make a medicinal tea for babies and nursing women
sangría	bloodletting
sarso	short wire lines on which to hang meat to dry
sierpe	serpent or large snake
susto	a folk disease related to fright
talache	digging and grubbing tool
tamales de elote	tamales made with fresh corn
tarima	a bunk or platform
tejer en gancho	crochet
temporada de la trasquila	sheepshearing season
tenasa	tree with straight, lightweight limbs used for roofing and to make jacal doors
tendajito	small store

151

tía y tío	aunt and uncle
tierra de agostadero	pasture land
tijeras tacincas	shearing scissors
tinaja	round hole dug beside a creek to divert or collect water
tipichil	pebble, sand, and lime mixture used for roofing
tocayo	namesake
toronjíl	lemon balm plant; leaves used to make tea
tortilla de maíz	corn tortilla
tren de carretas	cart train
tripas	intestines used as sausage casing
turcos	pastry made with a filling of ground pork meat, raisins, and nuts
valses	waltzes
venero	water vein, spring
vereda	track used to train horses
vigas	lumber beams
viznaga	barrel cactus
yerba buena	mint
yugo	yoke placed around the neck of an ox

Index

Pages containing illustrations appear in *italics*.

ISBN 1-58544-163-5

90000

9 781585 441631